3/24

The Spirit of Christ

THE SPIRIT OF CHRIST

By

FATHER JAMES, O.F.M.Cap.

M.A., Ph.D., B.D., D.Litt., Agrégé (Louvain),

Professor of Philosophy, University College, Cork.

THE NEWMAN BOOKSHOP

WESTMINSTER, MARYLAND

1945

Nibil Obstat: Fr. KIERANUS, O.F.M. Cap.

Censor Deputatus.

Imprimatur: ✠ DANIEL COHALAN,

Episcopus Corcagiensis.

22 / 9 / 1945.

First published October, 1945.

Printed in Ireland by Guy & Co. Ltd.

*In the mystery of the Incarnation
the descent of divine perfection
into the depths of human nature
is to be considered of greater
import than the ascent towards
God of human nature.*

SAINT THOMAS

111^a., Q.xxxiv, a.1, adl.

CONTENTS

Preface

PREFACE.

Two ways of life are open to every man. One is a mere casual existence in which he lives from hand to mouth with not a care for that vision which sees life whole and as a unity. Such a life is not worthy of a being endowed with mind whose thought, accepted by the will, should light up life and give it meaning. The other is constructive, affording an opportunity for a veritable art of living, the light of which is vision.

Here again two ways of life are possible. A man may elect to follow the light of natural reason and aim at a certain human dignity; or, he may hearken to the voice of God commanding him to a life that is more than human. To the credit of pagan thinkers be it said that when they spoke of human excellence, they glimpsed the fact that man, if he is to achieve it, must become "like to God." But it is Jesus Christ alone, sharing His Spirit with men by grace, Who makes it possible to live divinely in any real sense.

The entire aim of the Christian art of life is that docility to the designs of God which allows the Holy Spirit to fashion men anew in the image of Jesus Who is the unchanging Model of perfection. To this end the Spirit of Christ makes use of all the resources of human nature; He informs the soul with the divine life of grace; He adapts the human spirit in a permanent way to the delicacy of His mysterious initiatives. But as man, being free, resembles no other medium of creative Action, the Spirit of God requires from him a free response, an active consent of spirit, in the sedulous cultivation of a certain outlook: "For whosoever are led by the Spirit of God, they are the sons of God." [1]

The most important thing about a man, in effect, is a sure and settled outlook on the things that matter. Such an outlook is sometimes called a philosophy of life. G. K. Chesterton, for instance, was fond of saying: "There are some people, and I am one of them, who think that the most

[1] Roms., viii, 14.

important thing about a man is still his view of the universe."
This is eminently true, provided we realise that a man's
philosophy is simply the spirit in which he lives his life. The
choice, in fact, is not between having, or not having, a certain
spirit. Every man has his conception of life, his way of
viewing things, which is the spirit by which he lives. There
is, however, a choice of spirits. That is why Saint Paul is
able to narrow down the issue to this : "Now, we have
received not the spirit of this world, but the Spirit that is of
God : that we may know the things that are given us from
God." [1]

The following pages, from a longer work of which the
already published *Person of Jesus* formed a part, are but a
commentary on this inspired text and it is hoped that the
reader may be able, by the grace of God, to verify for himself
what the great Apostle has so forcibly written in another
place : "For the Spirit himself giveth testimony to our
spirit that we are the sons of God." [2]

FATHER JAMES, O.F.M.Cap.

In Festo Sancti Bonaventurae.

St. Bonaventure's,
   University Hostel,
      Cork.

[1] 1 Cor., ii, 12.
[2] Roms., viii, 16.

I.

Conversion.

I.

The life of holiness as it unfolds in history reveals three essential characteristics. There is, first, diversity within a unity, saint differing from saint, which is a witness to the intrinsic beauty of holiness. There is, secondly, a creative inspiration, giving power of influence to saints, which is altogether too impressive to be ignored. Finally, there is a process of conversion so uniform in its essentials that it points to important stages in the birth and growth of holiness. It is not too much to say, with history before one's eyes, that it is possible to recognise this divinest thing on earth and verify the truth of the completest summing-up of sainthood ever penned : " Now there are diversities of graces, but the same Spirit ; and there are diversities of ministries, but the same Lord ; and there are diversities of operations, but the same God, Who worketh all in all." [1]

These characteristics can be truly apprehended only from within the Church. To the rank outsider the spiritual life is only too often a dull monotony without originality, influence or adventure. The very heroes of our race, men and women who represent God's highest achievement in human form, are looked upon as negative, as devoid of colour as they are of life. From within, the vision is very different. Age and clime, temperament and sex, all those things which

[1] 1 Cor., xii., 4.

go to constitute historic men of flesh and blood spring into
relief to fill our minds with a wondrous vision. We see
humanity in the saints transfused by a common radiance,
the radiance of sanctity, and we see that radiance coloured
and diversified by the prism of human personality. And
because these men and women live, not far removed from us,
they may become our friends, our intimates, with whom our
commerce is as real, as personal, as the commerce we hold
with our contemporaries in the world of space and time.

The difference might be compared to that which exists
between viewing the stained-glass window of a church from
the outside and from within. From the outside the rays
of the setting sun may fall upon such a window, but they reveal
only a dull, uneven surface devoid of lustre or colour. Once
inside, however, things are very different. The self-same
window, dull and dark on the outside, has come to life, a
thing of rich and luminous colouring. Catching the rays of
the setting sun, it flings their pure white light in a veritable
spectrum of colours all around. And this is but a comparison
which, like all comparisons, illustrates one's meaning only
partially. But it does serve to suggest that the pure white
flame of sanctity, viewed from within the Church, appears
richly-coloured and luminous, taking its colour and relief
from the diversity of the saints. Sanctity is genius in
holiness. Essentially the same in all, it finds different
expressions in the life of different individuals. In the saints
alone is fully verified that magnificent image :

> *Life, like a dome of many-coloured glass*
> *Stains the white radiance of Eternity,*
> *Until Death tramples it to fragments.*

Besides diversity, there is a second characteristic of the
life of holiness which also compels attention. So recurring is
this characteristic in the life of the Church that it points to a
law of the spiritual life. The new power with which heroic
holiness invests certain saints becomes a spreading light.
This light pours out of them, invades and illumines others so

that around their persons, and under their inspiration, new beings are born into sanctity. Saints move down the path of history, the centre of groups. It is possible, in fact, to trace great onward surges in the life of the Church back to a single point, the transfiguration of some one individual man or woman. When this transfiguration in a complete surrender to the designs of God takes place, it is as if God bestowed upon such chosen ones something of His own creative power. Holiness then becomes a veritable conflagration which lights up the sky of particular epochs. That is why great historic movements in the past are largely the story of certain personalities chosen by God to be an inspiration and an example in His Church.

When we go on to ask history what it has to say about the origins of those men and movements, men and movements that have shaped the subsequent spiritual life in the Church, it points to a process so uniform that it may be ranked as normal in the rise of heroic holiness. This process is a real birth, a coming to new life, and is marked by a crisis called conversion. It would be a mistake to over-simplify this process, to think of it merely as a turning away from grave sin or infidelity, or to regard it as a thing finished once for all. Rather must we find in it just those elements which, in one form or another, are to be found associated with authentic holiness : first, active response to the initiative of God which is the true source of all conversion ; secondly, a new vision of the ideal in the light of which a man discerns his own sinfulness and imperfection ; thirdly, the awakening of desire for union with the Source of holiness in which true blessedness in life is seen to consist. Is it not as if in the midst of life a man receives a glimpse of the mysterious and haunting face of Holiness ? In the light of that vision he sees how far, as yet, he is from an ideal which seems to call him. The better to hear a Voice so intimate that it seems to speak within his breast he becomes, as it were, an exile and a pilgrim. Such a man may, or may not, go out from the haunts of men and cities but, in any event, he finds himself a stranger to things which before attracted him : he prays, and fasts, and waits until God has made known to him his precise vocation.

As we witness this recurring crisis in the lives of men, we are reminded that the Spirit of holiness is with the Church. It is the holy Spirit, the Spirit of Christ, Who reveals to men, in last analysis, the face of Holiness ; Who inspires men with a vivid sense of sinfulness and imperfection as a prelude to that illumination to be found in the imitation of Christ ; and Who awakens in them desire for that union with God which He alone can give. " In a true life of holiness," wrote St. Bonaventure, " there are three essential things : purification, the reward of which is peace ; illumination, the result of which is truth ; and union in which the soul receives the kiss of her heavenly Spouse." [1] These are the sublime gifts which await the man or woman who entirely surrenders to the pressure of God. They are conferred in what we can only describe as another Pentecost which sends forth a man from the solitude, in which it happens, to take up a fully energised and consecrated existence that will express itself in work no less than in prayer—and by which he renovates, in truth, the face of history.

II.

Outstanding proof of this and illustration are found in one man's dramatic conversion to Christianity after the death and resurrection of Jesus. It is the significance of Saint Paul that, though he was not an associate of Christ's earthly life, he reached that impassioned state of soul in which he could cry out : " For to me, to live is Christ." [2] So great was the repercussion of his conversion that it shook to its foundations the ancient house of Judaism and gave to the Church a man whose figure was to dominate the spread of the Christian Religion throughout the world. Paul had been marked out for the shafts of God's grace. Of him Jesus said : "For this man is unto me a vessel of election, to carry my name before the Gentiles." [3] That was the measure of Paul's vocation. From

[1] *De triplici via*, Prol.
[2] Phil. i, 21.
[3] Acts, ix, 15.

a sinner he became a saint ; from a persecutor of Christ he became Christ's great Apostle ; from a man blind to the truth of Christianity he became a prophet, inspired and enlightened and empowered to express, in texts that can never die, the purest essence of the Christian Spirit.

Saint John Chrysostom was of opinion that it were too little to call him Apostle ; he must be named another Christ. His bewildering versatility, his tireless energy, his terrific moral power dazzle us still as we read the record of his life. His writings have nourished minds in every age upon the things of the Spirit. What is more, as one listens to those great Letters in which he poured out the essence of his inner life one finds oneself, as it were, enveloped by a Presence. What Saint John Chrysostom, in his day, said of Paul is as true now as then : "While I listen carefully to the reading of Saint Paul . . . I exult with joy as often as I hear that spiritual trumpet ; and I am moved, and fired with zeal. For I recognise the voice of a friend and it is as if I saw him present and heard his voice."

This man who was destined to be an Apostle was unlike the Apostles that had lived with Jesus. There is no reason to think that he ever met the Master during the course of His earthly ministry. He says, in fact, that he never saw our Lord in the flesh. His friend and biographer, Saint Luke, has left us, in the Acts, an incomparable picture of his life and the startling events that composed it. Born at Tarsus of Cilicia, a little province on the north coast of Asia Minor, Saul, as he was then known, was reared in the strictest sect of Judaism ; he inherited a passionate hatred of the name of Jesus. Like other Jewish children he learned to read the Scriptures at his mother's knee ; and to complete his education he was sent to Jerusalem at the age of thirteen or fourteen. There his text-book would have been the Bible and he was initiated in the rigorist teaching of the school of Gamaliel. From this early education he emerged, he tells us, "a Hebrew, son of Hebrews, a Pharisee, a son of Pharisees," [1] that is, one whose whole mind was filled with anti-Christian prejudice.

[1] Cf. Phil. iii, 5 and Acts, xxiii, 6.

This prejudice was soon to manifest itself. The occasion was the martyrdom of Saint Stephen. Saint Stephen was one of the first deacons of the Church, a Greek-speaking Jew, who was bearing witness to the risen Christ. In his preaching he spared neither Pharisee nor Sadducee. He reminded them, as his Master before them had done, that it was the way of the stiff-necked Jews to persecute God's prophets. " Oh, you stiff-necked, you uncircumcised in heart and ears—you are the ones that resist the Holy Spirit : yea, even as your Fathers, do you. Which of the prophets did not your Fathers persecute ? Yea, they killed those who foretold the coming of the righteous one, and him in his turn you betrayed and murdered." [1]   That was a challenge to the authorities of the day and it proved too much for them. Rushing upon him, they heard him say : " I see the heavens opened, and the Son of Man standing on the right hand of God." [2]   Stephen was stoned to death. Driven to his knees before their onslaught, he prayed : " Lord, lay not this sin to their charge . . . " Standing on the outskirts of the mob, and holding the garments of the murderers, was the young man, Saul of Tarsus.

Upon him was destined to descend the grace of God's forgiveness. Had the prayers of the dying martyr reached his ears ? Had they made upon him some indefinable impression ? Or was it in answer to the prayers of Stephen that the grace of conversion came to Saul ? These are questions we cannot answer. Certain Fathers of the Church have indeed ascribed the conversion of Saul to the prayer of the first martyr for Christian Truth ; nor is it unlikely. The very fury with which Saul took up the persecution of the Christians is itself suspicious. A man will do many things, apparently contradictory, to stifle the first stirrings of conscience. What is certain is that this murderous episode, the guilt of which he shared, marks the real beginning of his career. He apparently made his way to the High Priest to offer his services for the work of exterminating the Christians. With the fiery zeal of youth he flung himself into the fight against the followers of Jesus Christ. He pursued

[1] Acts, vii, 51.
[2] Acts, vii, 55.

the Christians into their hiding-places and dragged them forth, men and women, delivering them up to be scourged. He wreaked his vengeance to the full upon the little Church at Jerusalem. Soon enough, except for the Apostles, Jerusalem was emptied of the Christians.[1] Dispersed in every direction, members of the little flock made their way even to distant cities. Many of them must have fled as far as Damascus.

The reactions of Saul to this exodus are not without their own peculiar interest. Jerusalem more or less emptied, Saul finds himself alone with his conscience ; and conscience is a disturbing thing. Was it to escape its incipient reproaches that he again plunges into the life of action ? The fact remains that he sought letters from the High Priest empowering him to carry his persecution beyond the confines of Jerusalem. Breathing out threats and slaughter, he set out to pursue at Damascus measures which had proved so successful in Jerusalem. This meant a journey of some seven or eight days and Saul equipped his caravan, taking with him a band of soldiers, to make the journey. This was to be the last act in the dramatic life of Saul. Mark it well. He has left behind him now the city of his success, he is on the road of destiny with time to reflect, and each new day, troubled probably by the goad of conscience, brought him nearer and nearer to the decisive moment of his life.

Just when Damascus, where he hoped to continue his persecution, loomed up before his view, the event occurs which transformed his whole life. It happened in this way. It was noon, when a light from heaven shone about him. More brilliant even than the Easter sun which blazed down upon the road in front of him, this new mysterious light struck Saul and his companions to the ground. The whole scene must have been bewildering. His companions were merely stunned. But Saul heard distinctly a Voice that spoke articulately to him, and in his own language : " Saul, Saul, why persecutest thou me ? Who art thou, Lord ? And he : I am Jesus whom thou persecutest. It is hard for thee to

[1] Acts, viii, 1.

kick against the goad.   And he, trembling and astonished, said : Lord, what wilt thou have me to do ?   And the Lord said to him : Arise, and go to the city, and there it will be told thee what thou must do." [1]

The conversation was brief.   But it was given to Saul to understand.   We find epitomised in it the history of all true conversion, however unspectacular to the outward eye, and hidden.   There is, first, the divine initiative of grace in a Voice that pleads, which even suggests that as the animal kicks against the goad to its own distress so must it be with the soul recalcitrant, and this Voice awakens in the soul of Saul a quickened consciousness of his past with its sinful persecution.   There is, secondly, the response of Saul who, hearing a Voice of majesty seeks first to discern its Source and then submissively offers to do his Master's Will.   There is, thirdly, a certain blindness to external things which is the beginning of a prolonged retreat.   When Saul was helped from the ground, it was found that he was blind.   He had to be led by the hand to the City.   There Saul found God's appointed prophet who baptised him and now as Paul he entered upon the most mysterious period of his life.   All we know is that he disappeared into Arabia,[2] and for some time no more is heard of him. We know, however, that in Arabia " he consorted not with flesh and blood," but left aside the ordinary affairs of life, entering that mysterious desert in which he received revelation from on high.   It was from the silence of this desert that the new man, Paul, returned to fill the ages with the lightning of his vision and the thunder of his voice.

III.

The better to appreciate this vision, which lights up the pages of the new Apostle's letters, it is necessary to advert a moment to the accounts of our Blessed Lord left us by eye-

[1] Acts ix, 4.
[2] Gal., i, 17.

witnesses of his life on earth. The parallel between men who came to Jesus as He preached His Gospel and the haughty Pharisee who knew Him not in the flesh is too significant to be ignored. These men, no less than Saul, received vocation and in response they were privileged to behold the light of heaven in the eyes of Jesus. But to each and all of them came the conviction of their weakness as they fled in the darkness that enveloped Calvary ; it was only at Pentecost, when the Spirit came, that they found strength to be living witnesses to Christ. It is impossible to draw aside the veil which hides from us the soul-searchings of Paul in the desert of Arabia. But when he comes forth, it is precisely with the vision of the men who had heard from the lips of Jesus the glad things of eternal life.

When Saint John, who was an intimate of the Master, has exhausted every effort to communicate his experience of Him, he brings his Gospel to an arresting conclusion with the words : " But there are also many other things which Jesus did ; which, if they were written down, every one, the world itself, I think, would not be able to contain the books that should be written." In no better way could " the Disciple whom Jesus loved " express his utter inability to tell the history of his Master. One has the definite impression that knowing Jesus was all that mattered and yet that in this living knowledge there are depths upon depths. The words and actions of our blessed Lord, the things He said and did, are so immense that no finite mind could grasp, much less utter, their real significance. They have passed into history to fill the centuries with their efficacy, to awaken minds to the grandeur of man's vocation, and to transform humanity into the image of its ideal, the Perfect, Jesus.

The Gospels were not written to give a complete account of our blessed Lord. There are characteristic differences between them and each Evangelist brings to his task a special preoccupation. It is not possible to read Saint Luke, for instance, without noting certain aspects of the sacred Infancy which are absent from Saint John. From the outset when Saint John soars aloft to contemplate the eternal generation of the Word while Saint Luke remains on earth to gather precious fragments concerning the Saviour's birth in time, the movement of their thought is different. This does not mean that Saint Luke, for all his human interest, intends to give a complete account of Jesus in the sense in which biography is commonly understood. The real aim of the Gospels is contained in the words of Saint John : " But these are written, that you may believe that Jesus is the Christ, the Son of God ; and that believing, you may have life in His name." [1]

However diverse the immediate purposes of the inspired writers, the central aim is the same in all. They are occupied with man's salvation, with the Kingdom of God in souls, with a doctrine of eternal life. It would be a mistake to imagine that such a doctrine is not relevant to the present time. For Jesus, Who is God, time and space do not exist : His eternity absorbs all time ; His immensity overflows all space. Salvation consists, as Saint John has said, in a saving faith in Jesus and his dictum takes its inspiration from the wondrous words spoken by the Master amidst the scenes of the Last Supper: " Now this is eternal life : that they may know Thee, the only true God, and Jesus Christ Whom thou hast sent." As there is no way of coming to the saving knowledge of God except through Jesus, this unity of inspiration, as manifest in the epistles of Saint John as in the exalted prayer of our blessed Lord, serves to bring into focus the scattered rays of light, thus giving to our religion the unity a central truth—the truth of Christianity which is Christ.

Exactly the same vision now fills the soul of Paul and in that elliptical style, so characteristic of him, he finds a single phrase in which to utter it. " For me," he says, " to live is Christ ; and to die is gain." At the source of such a phrase there is an eloquence, the eloquence of life itself, which is irresistible. To live for something—what does that mean ? It implies that a man has found within him a desire which is the deepest impulse of his life. There are men who live for the things of earth, for pleasure, wealth, ambition, self. But for the converted Pharisee the whole horizon of his mind is

---

[1] John, xx, 31.

filled with Christ Who is God and Man and in Whom, as in a living Centre, is found the whole mystery of creation, life and death.

But as there is no real attachment which does not involve detachment, no presence which does not create an absence, Paul finds himself a stranger to things he once held dear. Since for him to live is Christ, his life finds a new unity and centre around which henceforth his every thought and wish will gravitate. Because he has been drawn by God out of the death which was his former life, he is so captivated by his fellowship with Christ that he finds in his ardent soul but one ambition : "That I may know him, and the power of his resurrection, and the fellowship of his sufferings ; being made conformable to his death."

The power of Saint Paul so palpable in his writings derives from the uniqueness of his vision. This singleness of vision is the more impressive when we find it in a man who ranks with a Socrates, a Plato, a Seneca, and, above them, with Moses, greatest of Hebrew prophets, as one of the great spiritual teachers of humanity. Preaching before one of the most cultured audiences of the day, at Corinth, he declared his readiness to sacrifice everything, without exception, for this knowledge of Jesus Christ. In the strength of his vision he framed a mighty antithesis as true now as when he preached it : the twofold scandal of a Man Who is said to be God and of a God Who is said to be Man. The first is the scandal of the Greek which Paul designates " folly " ; the other is that of the Jew which a high-priest named "blasphemy." Without a victory over this two-fold obstacle all hope must be abandoned and the victory needed is not only of the head, but of the heart. A man must find in his soul, before he can accept Jesus and His salvation, that God-given humility which will enable him to say, with Saint John : "And we have known and have believed the charity, which God hath towards us."

Once this loving initiative of God is appreciated, a truth of vast significance awaits the attentive soul. Religion is not so much the pursuit of God by man as the pursuit of Man by God. Christianity, in particular, is the Word of God taking flesh and dwelling amongst men. Such is the prelude. But the real aim of our blessed Lord was to prepare the way for another coming, His coming in the Spirit. In this way He hopes to continue in humanity at large the life of love and praise which, in the name of men, He offered to the eternal Father in time. Just as, in life, He built up, day by day, the temple of His own humanity, so by the power of the Spirit He is engaged in building up that mystic Body, which we are, to the glory of the Father.

By no man was this more clearly seen than by Paul. For him life was bound up with Christ not only as an individual expression but in its social, its universal significance. For himself Paul could say : " I live, now not I, but Christ liveth in me." But in that very moment He could see that all humanity was to be the Body of Christ. In that moment, of supreme importance in the history of mankind, the universality of the Christian Religion was triumphantly affirmed. Saul had been a Jew of the Jews, but to Paul is given to announce the Gospel to the Gentiles and to proclaim that the Son of Man had come not only for the Jew but for every man of whom He is the Ideal and Prototype. But he could also say, having known the Law, that the Spirit of Christ alone could henceforth be the living Law of true perfection.

The surpreme contemporary fact is that men can become, by grace, what Jesus Christ is by nature, sons of God : " But as many as received him, he gave them power to be made the sons of God, to them that believe in his name." [1] That is why the Gospel is, as it were, an unfinished Gospel to be completed by those for whom the ideal is that expressed by Saint Paul : " I live, now not I, but Christ liveth in me." [2] Only when this is accepted by one's entire being will an eternal dream of God come true. That dream is a humanity remade " in the image and likeness of God." It comes into

[1] John, i, 12.
[2] Gal., ii, 20.

being when, by that mysterious identification of a man with Jesus, which is no obstacle to the self-identity characteristic of human personality, the signature of Jesus can be written to a man's every thought, desire and action. "I saw," said an eminent Mystic, "a great oneing betwixt Christ and us, for when He was in pain we were in pain. As long as He was passible He suffered for us and sorrowed for us ; and now He is uprisen and no more passible, yet still He suffereth with us." What this Mystic saw is that Jesus is born again in us, and lives in us, and that real holiness is nothing other than this continued Life by which daily He builds up His mystic Body to the full measure of God's designing, so that "doing the truth in charity, we may in all things grow up in Him who is the Head even Christ."

IV.

When one reflects upon the conversion of Saint Paul one will find an answer to a question which, at some time or other, has occurred to the mind of everybody. What is the difference that exists, even within the unity of the Church, between saints and sinners ? It cannot be denied, for instance, that Christians themselves are divided into those whose real ambition in life is sanctity and those who content themselves with less. Think of a Saint Francis of Assisi, a Blessed Angela de Foligno, a Saint Gemma Galgani. Compare with the heroism of their lives the apathy, or worse, of the vast mass of Christians in their day and ours. There is a difference. In what does it consist ? May we not say that the real difference lies precisely in the discovery of Christ ? Or to put the matter in another way. There are many who merely try to observe the Law of God ; there are others who have found the Person of Jesus. The difference may not, at first, seem great. But it is, in effect, the real chasm that separates men and women whose lives are ordinary, oscillating between sin and sanctity, never flowering in the heroism of sainthood, from those whose lives are entirely lightsome, advancing from grace to grace, increasing like the path of the just even unto perfect day. In the one case it is a

question of a law to be observed, a law for the non-observance
of which certain penalties exist ; in the other, there is intimacy
with a Person whose Presence is the atmosphere they breathe.

Reasons for this fundamental differences are not far
to seek. It is one thing to bend one's energies towards the
observance of a law ; it is quite another to love the lawgiver.
Those who endeavour merely to observe a law, who are
content not to violate it radically, sooner or later make the
sad discovery that law is a frail barrier between a man and
sin. What is needed is the Spirit of Christ, the instinct of
perfection, and that intimacy with Jesus which gives
undivided loyalty to the heart of a man or woman. When,
indeed, do men sin ? When they lose sight of Jesus. When
are men converted ? When the light of His countenance
falls upon the soul. For it is one thing to break a law ;
another to offend a Person. What is needed now, as in the
days of Saul, is the discovery of Christ Who meets men at
every cross-road in the journey of life. That is one reason
why the conversion of Saint Paul is of such significance.
It not only indicates the true source of the distinction between
sin and sanctity, but it reminds us that the discovery of Christ
by man is, in reality, the finding of man by Christ " yesterday,
and to-day ; and the same for ever." [1] Saul had no thought
of meeting Christ on the way to Damascus, but Christ came
to meet him. It is true that Saul must have been troubled
in soul before this and it would seem as if he had almost
stifled the voice of conscience. What we must not forget
is that Saul was blameless touching the ancient law. No man
observed it more rigorously. He took his place regularly in
the Temple ; he kept the Sabbath ; He was full of zeal for
Judaism. He was the very kind of man, one would have said,
who could not be converted. But converted he was. · No
man could have been more radically transformed. And it
happened simply because he was given a sight of Christ.
In that vision a man usually discovers what an imperfect
thing his life has been. No man could draw near to Jesus
and be content with a mere observance of the law. That
is a second thing to be learned from Saint Paul. It may be

[1] Hebr., xiii, 8.

comparatively easy to satisfy the rigid exigencies of the law, but it is impossible to exhaust the demands of God-given love for Jesus. Few realise what they are asking for when they pray for the love of God. Let it enter the heart as it did that of Paul, and there is no limit to be set to its ambitions. No sooner had Saul surrendered to Christ than he found within him the soul of an Apostle, the soul of a man who would lay down his life for the Cause of Christ.

There is a third, and final, thing we have to learn from Saint Paul. He was never satisfied with what he did ; hunger for perfection was strong within him. If we are inclined to think that his conversion was the end, and not the beginning of his life for Christ, his own words will quickly disabuse us. Conversion, to him, marked not only the end of an old life ; but the beginning of a new. His own avowal is touching and with it we may conclude this very imperfect sketch : " Not as though I had already attained, or were already perfect . . . But one thing I do ; forgetting the things that are behind, and stretching forth myself to those that are before, I press towards the mark." [1]

[1] Phil., iii, 12–15.

II.

Bethlehem.

I.

Of the many needs that agitate the human breast none is so profound as the desire of the heart for peace. The very word has power to stir in the soul's depths emotions that are literally inexpressible. It is as if some hidden wound, still open and bleeding, were touched by it ; a sigh escapes us for something we have lost or do not as yet possess. Day and night our hands stretch forth to the heights where, as we believe, the dwelling-place of peace is found. No effort seems too great, no fatigue too painful, for the ascent to her holy mountain. Where peace dwells, there also is achievement, happiness ; it is peace that man desires with all the ardour of his being.

A desire so profound must be instinctive and instinct is the authentic cry of life. Those who have listened to that cry, and heard its message, have looked to peace as the supreme thing sought by the tireless spirit of man. It is this very instinct which inspires all man's efforts and sustains him in these days of exile from a happiness of which he dreams. Peace represents that ultimate achievement which is the hope of the present with its fevers and anxieties ; through the prism of human tears, as in the clear white light of joy, it is the countenance of peace that is ever sought. In this sense desire for peace is the fundamental need of human nature ; it is the breath of life in every other desire. Every being

26

that sighs after a good unpossessed tends spontaneously towards its possession and seeks in that possession the absorbing quiet of repose. For that reason desire for peace is not just one amongst many claimants to our attention : it may be called the desire of desires which best expresses the deepest instinct of human nature.

So profoundly embedded in the human heart that it is instinctive, desire for peace is as universal as it is necessary. No man escapes the torment, or delight, of it. It may well be that men do not stop to think and reflect upon the tumult of desire that arises in their hearts. But the fact remains that all men, without exception, are in search of happiness. Now happiness and peace are indissolubly wedded. " It is not," says Saint Thomas, " that peace and bliss are quite identical but peace is related to happiness as an antecedent condition and a result which is a consequence." [1] Happiness is born of peace. The same impulse which takes man out from himself in search of happiness leads him towards the possession of peace which beckons from afar to every son of man. To this law there is not a single exception. All men, scattered as they are in space and time, are united in this common quest which, in some mysterious way, entices not only man but everything under the sun. It is as if some universal force were present in all things urging and impelling them towards a common destiny. The river sings her way between narrow banks to the ocean which calls ; the plant breaks through the sod in search of the sun's light which is its life ; the very birds upon the branches thrill with the joy of life and sing as they spread their wings in flight. Out from the heart of things comes, for those who listen, the music of an inspiration that runs through the things that are, that live, that know, until, within the mind of man, the music strives to become articulate in an overwhelming desire for peace.

A desire so profound and universal imparts a unity of direction to the many aspirations of the human spirit. It is true that all men, without exception, seek happiness and in

[1] II^a-II^ae, q.II, a.4, ad i.

that they are united. But where division comes, disturbing the very unity of mankind, is in men's choice of object, or ideal, of happiness. Without considering, for a moment, this diversity of opinion, there is a finding of ancient wisdom that is enlightening for our purpose. One of the great thinkers of antiquity, and indeed of all time, was the Greek philosopher, Aristotle. Among the many intuitive flashes of his genius there is one which is particularly illuminating. As he looked out upon the universe of things around him, which he saw with that penetrating glance of the true philosopher, it seemed to him that the universal secret was precisely the attraction exercised upon the world of reality by God, the First-Desired of all. Not that this attraction is clearly known to the world at large but there is in all things a soul of aspiration, a tendency to escape from their limitations and to enter, in some mysterious way, upon a pilgrimage that leads to God. God is, in fact, the unmoved Mover Who draws to Him, by a deep attraction, the entire universe of being in which man's position is privileged but not exclusive.

An intuition so magnificent, which orients the mind to God as to its true Centre, is a supreme witness to the power of human genius. "Life also belongs to God," wrote Aristotle, " for the actuality of thought is life, and God is that actuality." But Aristotle, it would seem, was blinded by the splendour of his own vision. He concluded that the very life of Godhead consists in thought, Thought of Thought as he phrased it, and from the nature of God he excluded love, at least where anything other than God is concerned. The God of Aristotle is the First-Desired of all creation, but His very perfection rules out not only knowledge of things changing and imperfect but the slightest interest in them that would ruffle the calm of His Self-contemplation. To the love which Aristotle found in all things, to the aspiration which is the breath of their life, to the invocation of imperfection, there is no response on the part of God ; the dew of peace does not descend from heaven. If we are to find traces of this new idea, the idea of self-giving and communication on the part of God, we must turn to a work which is not of human genius but of an inspiration that is divine.

II.

There is one concept absent from pagan thought or which, if it is present, never becomes the conscious possession of the pagan mind. That is the concept of creation in the light of which God appears not only in His transcendent majesty but as the unique Source of all that is. No necessity constrains God to draw things out of nothingness into being ; creation is a free act of love on His part. To the Hebrew people it was given to preserve, amidst the pagan polytheism of surrounding peoples, the idea of God, creative Source of things, and to realise, however dimly, that He is a God of love. It is true that in the history of this people there is a conflict between fear and love which was not without influence upon a true appreciation of the mystery of divine love. But it is impossible to read the pages of Sacred Scripture without a vivid conscious-ness of the chasm that lies between the revelation from on High and any other human document. In Plato for instance, as in Aristotle, we find a word for love (eros) which expresses the reaching out of man towards God. But it is only within the pages of revelation that we find that other word for love (agapé) which tells of God's approach to man. Granted that its occurrence is comparatively rare in the Old Testament, as compared with its frequent use in the New, the idea corresponding to it is there and is seeking expression in a thousand ways.

This people had, as other peoples also must have had, the memory of a state of things in which peace with God was the source of human happiness and of universal order. But this state of things did not last. When peace was disrupted and man became an exile from the Face of God he carried with him a promise of things to come which was to be his sole consolation in the exile to which rebellion drove him. Abraham was set aside by God and told : " I will make of thee a great nation, and I will bless thee and magnify thy name . . . and in thee shall all the kindred of the earth be blessed." But Abraham stands at the source of a people whose representative, Jacob, receives from God the further promise : " Thy name shall not be called Jacob, but Israel : for if thou hast been strong against God, how much more shalt thou prevail against men ? " [1] In time this change was made by God Himself and Israel, as a chosen people, entered upon her history of special association, and alliance, with God : " Thou shalt not be called any more Jacob, but Israel shall be thy name . . . Increase thou and be multiplied . . . and the land which I gave to Abraham and Isaac, I will give to Thee, and to thy seed after thee." [2] Of this alliance, or covenant, Moses was the official mediator and to seal the pact between Jehovah and Israel he offered sacrifice saying, as he sprinkled the people with the blood of the victims : " This is the blood of covenant which the Lord hath made with you concerning all these words." [3] From that moment, the word " covenant " or " alliance " re-echoes like a cry of hope and triumph from the pages of sacred Scripture.

That this alliance was entirely gratuitous on the part of God did not escape the consciousness of Israel : the love of God could not be forced. Israel saw herself as the object of God's predilection and the awareness of her many infidelities did but increase the wonder of it. Ezechiel recalls to her the day of her birth when, cast upon the earth, she was trodden under foot until the Lord God came and took notice of her : "And I passed by thee, and saw thee : and behold thy time was the time of lovers : and I spread my garment over thee, and covered thy ignominy. And I swore to thee, saith the Lord, God : and thou becamest mine." [4] Not to Ezechiel alone came the word of God but to prophet after prophet came the revelation of the God of love, and of His zealous love for this people of His choice. On the lips of Osee the alliance is a nuptial union in which Jehovah has taken Israel for His bride ; [5] in the *Canticle of Canticles* the same theme is sung in matchless beauty ; and Israel has the assurance that God has the heart of a mother for His chosen people : " Can a woman forget her infant, so as not to have pity on the son of her womb ? And if she should forget, yet will not I forget thee." [6]

[1] Gen., xxxii, 28.
[2] Gen., xxxv, 10–12.
[3] Exodus, xxiv, 8.
[4] Ezech., xvi, 8.
[5] Osee, x, 1.
[6] Is., xlix, 15.

This special association of God with Israel looked to the future for its culmination. The eyes of Israel are fixed upon distant horizons, her dreams transcend the passing moment ; she looks forward to an era in which alliance with God will bear appropriate fruit in peace. There are times when Israel's reading of that future is disturbed by visions of mere material prosperity, but in her inspired moments she really sees that her true destiny is to be the source of God's peaceful triumph over human souls. This is particularly true of the second part of the book of Isaiah which, instead of calling down upon the Gentiles the chastisement of God, invites them rather to the recognition of the truth. " It is a small thing," said Jehovah to the Messiah of the future, " that thou shouldest be my servant to raise up the tribes of Jacob and to convert the dregs of Israel. Behold, I have given thee to be the light of the Gentiles, that thou mayst be my salvation even to the farthest part of the earth." [1]

In this text there is reference to the anointed One, the Messiah, Who would realise on earth the kingdom which is the object of Israel's hopes and aspirations. It would be impossible here to collect the many references to the Messiah. He appears upon the pages of the Old Testament in many forms, now as the servant of Jehovah, now as the Son of Man, and there is a reference to the Son of God. [2] But in general He is the " anointed One," the Messiah, and He is destined to spring from the house of David. The place of His birth, Bethlehem, is foretold by the prophet, Michaeas, and Isaiah has what is perhaps the best description of Him : " For a child is born to us, and a son is given to us, and the government is upon his shoulder : and his name shall be called Wonderful, Counsellor, God the Mighty, the Father of the world to come, the Prince of Peace." [3]

This hope of Israel inspired by God gives momentous impetus to her sacred history and she is carried by it towards the advent of the " Desired of all nations." But the hope

[1] Is., xlix, 6.
[2] Ps., ii, 7.
[3] Is., ix, 6.

itself is not so entirely lightsome that it excludes the obscurity of misinterpretation.   It would seem that the very centre of it, the Divinity of the Messiah, escaped the comprehension of the people, as if God were reserving for the actual moment of realisation the manifestation of His design.   As Judaism is about to complete its history the messianic hope is very much alive in Palestine.   From the background emerge a number of chosen souls who, despite the fact that the voice of prophecy has been stilled for a long time, are ready for God's final revelation.   There is Zachary, father of the man who is to prepare the way ; there is within the precincts of the Temple a Simeon and the widow, Anna, who are living in expectation ; there is at Nazareth the very Flower of Israel, Mary.   As one stands upon the brink of this mysterious period, which is the " fulness of time," one can almost hear the wings of time fluttering with impatience for that consummation which is the meaning of universal history.   Saint Paul, with the actual realisation of God's design before his mind, sums up that history in a few words : "God, who at sundry times and in divers manners, spoke in times past to the fathers by the prophets. last of all, in these days hath spoken to us by His son, whom he hath appointed heir of all things, by whom also he made the world." [1]   But the mystery which gives meaning to this brief statement has yet to be accomplished.

III.

The propitious hour has now arrived and God is about to give effective realisation to the hopes which, for centuries, He has breathed into the heart of Israel.   To do so He, Who is no respector of persons, passes by the rich, the known, the powerful, the chiefs of the people both religious and political, and He chooses a humble maiden, Mary, in the little village of Nazareth.   She is, in truth, the one soul on earth upon whom, the gaze of God rests in loving complacency ; in her alone does He find repose.   To Mary He sends his angel and is pleased to await upon her consent : " The Holy Ghost shall come upon thee, and the power of the Most

[1] Hebr., i, 1.

High shall overshadow thee. And therefore also the Holy which shall be born of thee shall be called the Son of God."[1]

This was the Child of whom Isaiah had foretold that He should be the fruit of virginity ; the Child Who could be fashioned only by the Holy Spirit ; the Child over Whom the Spirit should have full sway to pour into His human soul the priceless gifts of God. "And there shall come forth a rod out of the root of Jesse ; and a flower shall rise up out of his root. And the Spirit of the Lord shall rest upon him : the spirit of wisdom, and of understanding, the spirit of counsel, and of fortitude, the spirit of knowledge, and of godliness. And he shall be filled with the spirit of the fear of the Lord."[2] The young maiden, already so much in the grace of God, now listens and as vistas are opened up before her eyes she gives consent to the request of God with every fibre of her immaculate being. In that instant the mystery of the Incarnation is accomplished. "While all things were in the quiet silence and the night was in the midst of her swift course thine almighty Word leaped down from heaven out of thy royal throne."[3] On earth there was peace at last in heaven's wedding with the soul of Mary the fruit of which is the Prince of Peace.

Mysteriously enough there was a kind of external peace at this moment and the Roman authority, Caesar Augustus, availed of it a few months later to make a census of the entire country. His edict to that effect was published. It was necessary for Mary to depart from Nazareth with her husband, Joseph. Joseph was of the family of David, and Bethlehem, of which Michaeas had spoken, was the City of David to which Joseph had to repair for inscription. The hour was ill-chosen for Mary whose time approached for the birth of her Child. The pride of Emperors is not likely to take account of such things and even Emperors, in their pride, are in the Hands of God. The idea of a census for Palestine may have been conceived by Tiberius for many reasons ; but

[1] Luke, i, 35.
[2] Is., xi, 1–3.
[3] Wisdom, xviii, 14, 15.

nothing could prevent him from being an instrument for the realisation of God's prophecy. "And thou, Bethlehem Ephrata, art a little one among the thousands of Juda : out of thee shall he come forth unto me that is to be the ruler in Israel : and his going forth is from the beginning, from the days of eternity." [1]

For Mary and Joseph, however, it meant a journey of three or four days from Nazareth to the City of David. The rich made such a journey in chariots ; the poor on foot. Tradition cannot then be far wrong in picturing Mary seated on a humble ass, accompanied by Saint Joseph on foot, with staff in his hand, and some slight provisions. The route to be followed was that taken three times a year for the Feasts in Jerusalem. Reaching Jerusalem, they were but a two hours journey from the City of David. The whole journey was a difficult one. Disappointment awaited them at the end of it. Many of their compatriots had gone before. Bethlehem, when they arrived, was crowded. There was no room for them in the inn. It was a pathetic group, the young maiden about to be a mother, with the anxious man at her side, wandering in the streets of Bethlehem in search of shelter. Night was quickly falling ; Mary's hour approached. But there was no shadow of anxiety on Mary's countenance. She carried with her the Desired of all nations, the God Who is omnipotent and omniscient, and to be worried on His behalf would not have been worthy. She could not find it in her heart to envy other mothers more comfortably situated. She was Mother of Him Who would save humanity and in her present suffering she found joy : that she should in this way enter upon her role as co-redemptress ; and that she should thus be carrying the Cross by bearing Him Who finally would be stretched upon it. She followed Joseph through the crowded streets of Bethlehem without fear, without anxiety, and when their searching ended in a stable of poverty Mary was content. This content had been stealing over her this lastwhile ; drop by drop the peace of heaven was entering her soul ; she could feel the beating of the little Heart within her and found assurance ; the darkness stealing

[1] Mich., v, 2.

out of the night held no terrors for her ; she found it necessary
to hide beneath her modest eyelids the joy that was surging
in her soul . . . The ecstatic moment had at last arrived.
Mary gave to the world the Child of Bethlehem Who is at
once the Son of Man, the fruit of her own virginity, and the
Son of God Whose eternal Birth in the bosom of Godhead
now finds mysterious completion in the Birth of time.

At that moment heaven's portals opened and the night
was filled with the song of peace. As if to reward the
Shepherds, whose flocks had vacated the stable in which
Jesus was born, they were privileged to hear the voice of heaven
in the night. You can see them with their black veils upon
their heads, their miserable tunic bound around them, and the
sheepskin on their shoulders, watching and minding their
flocks when suddenly they were awakened by heaven's *Gloria*
in the skies. "And behold an angel of the Lord stood by them,
and the brightness of God shone about them, and they feared
with a great fear. And the angel said to them : Fear not ;
for, behold, I bring you good tidings of great joy, that shall
be to all the people. For this day is born to you a Saviour,
who is Christ the Lord, in the city of David. And this shall
be a sign unto you : You shall find the infant wrapped in
swaddling clothes, and laid in a manger. And suddenly
there was with the angel a multitude of the heavenly army,
praising God, and saying : Glory to God in the highest :
and on earth peace to men of good will." [1]

The shepherds arise and find their way to the little
shelter beneath the rock. Bethlehem sleeps, unconscious of
the great Mystery that has happened in its midst. But then
Bethlehem had found no room for the advent of Jesus. Only
the shepherds enter in and pay homage to their God in
human form whose only altar is a humble manger.

IV.

The mind's first reaction to such an Event is one of wonder,
a wonder that is akin to hopeless incomprehension. But it is

----

[1] Luke, ii, 9–14.

impossible to rest in that. The light of Faith shining in the mind pierces the darkness with which pride would meet the mystery of the Incarnation. But let the charm of the Child of Bethlehem work its spell on a humble mind and it is marvellous to watch how the darkness of Mystery offers increasing light to the mind. It is related that Saint Francis of Assisi built a crib at Greccio in order to celebrate Bethlehem. In his loving arms, with the light of heaven around him, the Child came to life and it was a living Child he placed in the empty manger. Those who stood around were struck by the miracle which Jesus worked for him who loved so well. But is there not something deeper ? Love is reciprocal. If Francis loved Jesus, and found his joy in Him, it was precisely because Jesus loved Francis and found peace in His arms. But the Child that Francis held in his arms had, in truth, been conceived in Faith by Francis, just as He had been born in Francis of the Charity in his heart and brought forth in his life in works that were not only of Francis but of Christ with whom, in the Spirit of God, he was united.

It is impossible, in fact, to reflect upon the desire for peace, and that new form of it awakened in Israel, without a glimpse into the very deepest truth in life. Man finds himself in search of peace, and implicitly, of God in Whom the happiness of man is stored. But this search for peace is simply a response, a response on the part of man to God's quest for him. This is true not only in the supernatural order where the initiative of God is so clearly marked but on the infinitely lower plane of nature, where God Who is the creative Source of things is, by the very fact, their ultimate End and Purpose. Creation is itself an act of love, gratuitous and free, in which God not only calls into being the things that are and then orients them towards a perfection which is a reflection of His own, but the very act of creating, inspired by love, is a drawing of things from nothingness into that embrace of love which is their being. It follows that, even on this level, the aspiration of the human spirit is the inspiration, in another form, of the love which prompts God to share with nothingness the reflected glory of His Being.

We must pause, however, if we would measure something of the abyss which lies between creation as a work of love and the tremendous intimacy of the Incarnation in which the Son of God takes unto Himself our human nature. It is much to know that God exists, greater still to adhere, as the Israelites did, to the unity of God. But before the Mystery of God both man and angel must bow down in humblest adoration. There is but one God. And had God not chosen to make known His inner life, shared as it is by Three divine Persons, we should never have known what goes on within the bosom of Godhead. The reason is not far to seek. The three Persons are distinct one from the other only by relations of origin within the unity of Godhead ; all things else, nature and perfection and activity, they possess in common. There is, in reality, only one God. Every time there is a manifestation of the power of God, as in creation, the three Persons act as One and it is precisely this Unity which hides and veils from every created mind the inner Mystery of Godhead. No creature, be he man or angel, could hope to scale the heights, surprise the secret of God's inner life, and return to himself enriched, being " like to God." But that limitation does not exist for God ; He could reveal Himself for what He is, the Triune God. And that is what happened. One of the divine Persons, the Word, took unto Himself man's nature and made it share in the dignity of His own divine Personality. We who have been brought up in the Faith find ourselves saying this as if it were the most ordinary thing in the world. But pause a moment and try to see what it means. A created being has been taken into the very triune Life of Godhead. A created nature is now possessed by the Person of The Word. The result is that this created nature now enjoys relations to the Father which are also the relations of the Son and consequently is associated with the Father in that relation by which Father and Son breathe forth the Spirit. The Humanity of Jesus is thus united to the Word in a union which is hypostatic or personal and has entered into the bosom of Godhead to share in this intimate Life of Godhead so jealously reserved to the Three divine Persons. Jesus is " one of the Three " as the traditional formula of the Faith

has it : He is the Son of the Father : He is with the Father the
Source of the Holy Spirit.

How then can we estimate the ecstacy of love which lies
at the source of the Incarnation ?   Saint Thomas saw the
point so clearly that a text from him has been the inspiration
of these pages.   " In the Mystery of the Incarnation," he
wrote, the descent of divine Perfection into the depths of
human nature is to be considered of greater import than the
ascent towards God of human nature ?" Who indeed could
bridge the gulf between finite nature and infinite Godhead
save God Himself ?   That is the wonder of the Incarnation
which reveals to us the stupendous fact that God is not only
Pure Act, Thought of Thought, but a God for Whom Saint
John could only find the word agape, love, because in Him the
Godhead is expressed not only by way of generation in the
Son Who is the Wisdom of the Father, but in the Spirit Who
is the Love in which Father and Son are united.   And if the
Act of the Incarnation is the act of God as One, the term of
that Act is the Only-Begotten of the Father ; just as it is by
the power of the Holy Spirit, the Spirit of Love, that the
mystery is enacted in the Virgin Mary.

With this knowledge of the Triune God in mind, Saint
Thomas was able to see that the ultimate reason for creation
itself must be sought within the Godhead.   He finds it in the
eternal processions of the three divine Persons within the
unity of Godhead.   Creation is called the temporal procession
of things from God and on this account we speak of God as
creative Source.   But since God made all things in Wisdom,
the generation of the Son is the cause and reason for the
production of things in creation so that the love of the Father
for the Son is the deep source of all God's self-communication.
Thus it is that the Holy Spirit, the love by which the Father
loves the Son, is also the love by which He loves the creature
bestowing upon it His perfection.

Bethlehem exercises upon the mind a fascination that is
inescapable.   It reminds us of a triple birth : the eternal
birth of the Word of God ; the birth in time of the Word

made flesh ; and the mystic birth in the souls of Christians of Jesus Who is the Prince of Peace. The Church encourages us to look at Bethlehem in this way : she celebrates at Christmas, this triple birth in her three Masses. Through the mouth of Isaiah God had said : " Shall not I that make others to bring forth children, myself bring forth, saith the Lord ? Shall I, Who give generation to others, be barren, saith the Lord thy God . . . You shall be carried at the breasts and upon the knees they shall caress you. As one whom the Mother caresseth so will I comfort you." [1] Peace, like love, is reciprocal. Let a man find peace in God and God finds His peace in him. And if, mystically, a child is re-generated so that he shares, by grace, in the Sonship of Jesus then, by that same supernatural birth, Jesus is mystically born in the soul of a child. Who shall grant us the heart of child that Jesus may find another Bethlehem from which to set forth in the world of space and time on His mission of peace ?

[1] Is., lxvi, 9–13.

III.

Nazareth.

I.

It is a first principle of the spiritual life that meditation on the Person of Jesus is the living source of authentic holiness. In this meditation the mind is enlightened, the heart is inflamed, and there are moments when, contemplating the Word Incarnate, the devout soul is intoxicated with incomparable delight. " Not the sweetness of honey," said Saint Bonaventure, " nor the odour of the most exquisite perfume can compare with the delight of contemplating Jesus." This contemplation not only consoles the human spirit with its sweetness but fortifies with its strength and ultimately, by that reciprocal efficacy of love, transforms the whole man into the likeness of its Object, Jesus Christ.

There are many mysteries of our blessed Lord which possess this intrinsic power of transformation. Just because He is the God of each, recognising the uniqueness of human personality, He offers Himself in His many mysteries, and within each mystery in the infinitude of His attraction, so that there is diversity of appeal within the unity of the life of the spirit. There are some who respond to the majesty of Jesus as He preaches on the hill-side His doctrine of eternal life ; there are others who are touched by the pathos of Him as He sinks beneath the weight of the world's sinfulness in the Garden of Gethsemane. But there is one portion of His life on earth which draws us by the very mystery of it, that

portion which we designate the hidden life. The glory of
an hour that shone about the cradle of His birth has
disappeared, the Star that led the Magi to Bethlehem has
ceased to shine, and Jesus is lost in the obscurity of common
life, an obscurity that stretches from childhood to youth,
from youth to manhood, only to cast its shadow far into His
public life on earth.

It is clear that Jesus, Son of God, could have fashioned
from the very earth a Body and appeared before men in the
full stature of His manhood. Had He done so, proclaiming
from heights of magnificent isolation His doctrine of eternal
life, we should have no reason for complaint : such a mission
would have been in keeping with the majesty of Godhead.
But that He should have been born of woman a little child,
that He should have submitted to childhood's touching
helplessness, that He should have grown up, in everything
like unto the Son of Man, finally to emerge from the narrow
circle of a human family is calculated not only to touch the
heart but to inspire the mind with longing to penetrate the
mystery of it. Why, indeed, did Jesus elect to be born of
woman, to receive from Mary that mother-love than which
nothing more beautiful exists on earth. Why, from heaven's
heights, and from an eternal generation did He descend to
be begotten in time and commence His life on earth in utter
dependence upon a human mother ? Why was He, the very
Son of God, content to hide His identity beneath the
protecting shadow of a foster-father ? Why did He, Who is
Lord of the world, make Himself dependent for human
sustenance upon the humble labours of the carpenter, Joseph ?
Why did He so resolutely reject all that the world values, the
wealth for which men toil, the renown for which men work,
the idle leisure for which they live ? Why, in a word, did
Jesus so arrange His existence in our midst that for almost
thirty years He led a life that was unknown, hidden, obscure ?

These are questions that well up spontaneously in our
minds before the spectacle of the hidden life. They are not
idle questions, for they touch the deepest purposes of the
Incarnation. A first answer to them might be sought from a

little text that is repeated no less than five times in the second chapter of Saint Matthew. The text is this : "And entering into the house they found the Child with Mary His Mother." The text directly refers to the Magi's finding of our blessed Saviour but it is so entirely congruous that it might be taken to sum up their relations in time as in eternity. Were they not, by a unique decree, inseparable in the Mind of God ? Are they not, in fact, as inseparable as Reality and Reflection ? What more fitting than the merging into one of destinies that were alike ?   One has only to think in order to realise that, as the Child grew up in grace and strength beneath the mother's loving care, each new manifestation of the Divine life within the human, which She gave, was a grace for her. Destined by God to perfect creaturehood, marvellously receptive to the virtue that went out from Him, Mary had beneath her eyes the living Model of perfection in whose Presence she would reach the heights of heroism intended for her. Nowhere, in fact, is the union of the Child and Mother, of Mother and Child, so constant and continuous as in the common light of day which is this mysterious period.

Nothing is less idle, however, than contemplation. The mysterious union of Child and Mother which allows the mind so easily to pass from one to the other is enigmatic. Suddenly this very hidden life sets the fuse to holy speculation. Just when we should have expected the union to continue, it is broken, broken at least on the surface. There is a separation, the anguish of which we can only dimly surmise, which comes in this hidden life as a sudden apocalypse of divine intentions, and just as suddenly the veils of obscurity are drawn back again. Just when the mind had found heaven on earth in the shape of a human family, the spell is broken. Why had this to be ? Why, in circumstances eminently mysterious, with no conceivable fault on the part of Joseph and Mary or Jesus, had the little home to suffer a loss that plunged the sword of sorrow deep into the heart of the most sinless creature that ever lived ?

The more we study Christian Origins the more we realise that Christianity is an action, a way of life, before it is a formal doctrine. At the source of everything lies the Act of God which is the Incarnation. Until we have begun to surmise the significance of that Act, we cannot hope to understand the very formulae by which we express our religion. It is just the beauty of this portion of the Master's life that it forces us to reconsider the situation. Saint John, for instance, is emphatic that the very touchstone of our Faith is the ability to accept the stupendous fact that God is Love. "And we have known," he says, " and have believed the charity which God hath to us." This was, in fact, the revelation of our Lord to humanity. Saint John clearly saw it and was for ever emphasising it. " By this hath the charity of God appeared towards us, because God hath sent his only begotten Son into the world, that we may live by him." [1] But what is the real significance of this ? It is the social nature of the Godhead. God is not the unique Being of whom philosophers like Aristotle dreamed, but the One within whose Unity there is this ineffable communication of life, this sharing of Divinity by Three Persons. Now our blessed Lord, the Son, is not only Son of God but Son of Mary, so that He Who is the Second Person of the Holy Trinity is also Member of a human family. But, in ordinary relationships, the bride of the son belongs to the family of the father. It follows that Mary, Who is Mother as well as Bride, is already taken into the society of Godhead, and through her, the man who is wedded to her. We find ourselves, therefore, in presence of a human family which is not only an image of the Holy Trinity but which, mysteriously, is taken up into the society of Godhead here on earth.

To Jesus belongs the task of this elevation of a human family to the heights of Godhead. He is the Son begotten by the Father. His aim is to inaugurate on earth the life of heaven. He is, in fact, the new Beginning so that from the bosom of a human family He will return to the Father the love of which he is the bearer to mankind. His aim is to share this Sonship, by grace, with men, to introduce them into the society of Godhead. Now just because He is a new

[1] 1 John, iv, 9.

Beginning, One over whom the Spirit of God will have complete empire, He sets Himself in diametrical opposition to the Spirit of the world.   He is the Truth of God made manifest and the truth is that God is Love.   To Blessed Angela de Foligno our Lord once said : " See if there be aught else in me but love."   "And my soul," notes Angela, " comprehended with great certainty that He was naught else but Love." Because He loved, He chose that form of life in which love's choicest human virtues   are   made   manifest—the   humility which stoops, the patience which suffers, and the obedience which is faithful.   If we would find these virtues in all the dazzling purity of their splendour we must see them against the background of Nazareth.

The atmosphere that surrounds Nazareth in the pages of the Gospel is one of breathless silence.   So silent is Nazareth that it seems almost rash to speak of it.   From another point of view this silence is dark, dark as if the Holy Spirit wished to curtain off the growth of Jesus from the eyes of men. Bethlehem, Egypt, Nazareth seem to be so many steps by which the Son of God descends, and is finally engulfed, in an abyss of silence and darkness.   We do not know for certain the length of time He passed in Egypt, away from Herod's anger, and when Saint Joseph returned to Judea it was to find Herod's son reigning there.   "Arise, and take the child and his mother," the Angel had said, " and go into the land of Israel.   For they are dead that sought the life of the Child." [1] Fearing lest the son might prove like his father, Joseph " retired into the quarters of Galilee." [2]   Now Galilee was a province which, at that time, was rather an object of disdain— Galilee of the Gentiles, it was called—and in Galilee the humblest, the most insignificant town was Nazareth.

Far from the throbbing life of the great city of Jerusalem, Nazareth was just a little village lost amongst the hills of Galilee, hills that encircled it and cut it off from the great high roads of public commerce.   The guileless Nathanael expressed the common opinion of the day when, in wonder,

[1] Matt., ii, 20.
[2] Ibid. ii, 22.

he asked : " Can anything of good come from Nazareth ? "
No great Rabbis had come from Galilee, and Nazareth, without
even a school which was the pride of every Jewish town, was
not expected to contribute to the religious movements that
agitated Jerusalem. Nazareth was, indeed, a secure retreat
hidden away from the eyes of men. Nazareth simply waited,
waited to become the most sacred place on earth, the home
where Jesus would continue the salvation that had begun
therein until the moment came to carry it beyond the encircling
hills into the vast world that lay beyond.

Nazareth means darkness but it is a darkness of excessive
light. When we reflect, forgetting the more human estimate,
we begin to see it for what it is. Saint Jerome in a phrase
of great beauty speaks of Nazareth as the Rose of Galilee
which opens its petals only to the gaze of heaven. That is the
literal, though divine, truth. It was at Nazareth that heaven
found the Flower of Israel, Mary, and it was at Nazareth that
salvation for mankind began in that perfect phrase : " Be it
done unto me according to thy word." No sooner was this
phrase uttered than the Word was made flesh and the Son of
God made man declared His mission : " Sacrifice and
oblation thou wouldst not : but a body thou hast fitted to me.
Holocausts for sin did not please thee. Then said I : behold
I come : in the head of the book it is written of me : that I
should do thy will, O God." [1] Never had earth offered such
music before the great white Throne of God as when these
two selfless human Voices, in unison, pronounced the saving
words : " Be it done unto me according to thy word." There
was a hush in the courts of heaven. Angels listened to praise
that was not merely human but divine. The source of that
great music, to utter which the world was made, was Nazareth
amongst the hills.

It was not for His own sake that Jesus came on earth.
He came to give Himself. To whom ? In the first place
to the eternal Father Whose Son He was. It is important
to emphasize this if we are to have a proper understanding of
Jesus. In the bosom of the Godhead the Word is the praise

[1] Hebr. x, 5.

and glory of the Father ; on earth His whole desire is to be the same. Jesus is what He is precisely because He is the Word, the Expression of the Father, and He has come on earth so that in Him, and by Him, all creation shall return to God, its real Source. This love of His, this gift of a divine Self now made by Him in human terms, in human nature, is itself the beginning of redemption and consequently His essential work on earth. Is He not our Ransom ? Is He not the Price of our sinfulness ? Is He not our Priest, our Mediator, the Voice that cries to God from our humanity which He assumed : " Behold I come : in the head of the book it is written of me, that I should do thy will, O God."

It is true that when the time comes He will go forth, He will preach, and He will suffer death but all these actions, magnificent as they are, simply express the one fundamental thing : " Behold, I come to do thy will, O God." That cry, in the night of the world, is the very reality of Jesus, at every moment of His life, at Nazareth as well as upon the Cross, in the tabernacles of our Church as upon the hill of Calvary. And it is this which explains the mysterious incident which was the solitary interruption of the hidden life at Nazareth.

Jesus found Himself, a Child of twelve, in the Temple of His Father at Jerusalem. It is probable that this was not His first visit to Jerusalem but special significance attaches to this one because, at the age of twelve, a Jewish boy was bound to the observation of all the precepts of the Law : Jesus had now become a Son of the Law. It is not difficult to surmise the emotions that He welcomed as He found Himself in the sacred place. God Himself had planned the Temple ; His Law was there ; its very walls echoed with the praise of centuries. Streams of blood had flowed from sacrifices offered here ; columns of incense had ascended to the Most High ; God had filled the House, on occasion, with the power of His Presence. And Jesus now is there. It is a moment when the Father witnesses to Him. Soon He is surrounded by a group of people. Their looks are concentrated on Him. "And all that heard him," says Saint

Luke, "were astonished at his wisdom and his answers," [1]
We are told explicitly that amongst those onlookers there
were "doctors" of the Law. Just at this moment a young
woman, accompanied by a man, appear. They are visibly
affected. But at the sight of Him in the midst of the doctors
they too are astonished. They listen on the fringe of the
group. Immediately He rejoins them. Mary says : "Son,
why hast thou done so to us ? Behold thy father and I
have sought thee sorrowing." It was then that Jesus witnessed
explicitly to the Father in words that may well be taken as
the text of His whole life : "Did you not know that I must be
about my father's business ?" In Jerusalem, or at Nazareth,
it was the same : the desire of Jesus was to do the Will of God.

John the Baptist had, on one occasion, declared : "I
am the voice of one crying in the wilderness." But Jesus is
not only the voice but the very Word of God in humanity
crying to God. All that He is, all that He does, all His
thoughts and sentiments and aspirations, every sigh and
gesture, every joy and sorrow, all the pulsations of His human
Heart amd every breath of His Being, all are part of one
great cry to God. At any moment you could have gone to
Jesus and found that it was so—to the Child in the cradle,
the great Preacher on the hillside, or the King on His throne
on Calvary. But at Nazareth there is, as it were, nothing
else. Like Moses, lost in the cloud, His converse is with
God alone.

It is not possible for long to entertain this thought without
seeing the humble home of Nazareth transfigured before one's
eyes. The cloud which envelops it grows luminous, the
veils that surround it seem to fall aside, and Nazareth becomes
the sanctuary of the Real Presence. The little hills
surrounding it are like hooded monks at prayer. The lights
that flicker in the darkening sky are candles lit by angel-hands.
One almost hears the air quivering with angel-music and then
one kneels before the golden Monstrance of a little Child
to unite with Him, in the company of two silent personages,
Mary and Joseph, in offering to the eternal Father the world

[1] Luke, ii, 47.

beyond that is lost in the darkness of sin and ignorance.
Nazareth is then a Tabernacle.

III.

In the life of Mary and Joseph, who lived by Faith, the
loss of Jesus is of such supreme significance that it sheds light
upon a recurring fact in the history of man's search for God.
In the hearts of both, from the moment they became aware
of their loss, there was but a single question : "Where is
Jesus ? " He has disappeared, as suddenly as when in later
years He escapes through the ranks of His enemies. He has
gone. It is not difficult to surmise their anguish and there is
not a soul with slightest experience of His ways, who will not
say : "Whither is thy beloved gone, O thou most beautiful
among women ? Whither is thy beloved turned aside, and we
will seek him with thee ? " [1] It is ever best to set out in
Mary's company if one would find the Beloved : She under-
stands what it is to be deprived of Him. " I opened the bolt
of my door to my beloved : but he had turned aside, and was
gone. My soul melted when He spoke. I sought him, and
found him not : I called, and he did not answer me." [2] On
the third day Mary with Joseph finds her Son; the night is over.

After this incident of the loss of Jesus, and His subsequent
finding in the Temple, Saint Luke sums up the life at Nazareth
in this cryptic text : "And he went down with them, and came
to Nazareth, and was subject to them." With one other
remark, which he repeats twice, this Evangelist, so interested
in the details of the Master's life, concludes the second Chapter
of his Gospel and in the third begins the public life of our
blessed Lord. The detail he repeats concerns the growth
of Jesus : first, when he relates the return to Nazareth ;
second, when he tells of the finding in the Temple. " And
Jesus," he says, " advanced in wisdom and age, and grace with
God and men." The veil of silence has again descended
upon the life of Jesus and nothing could be more significant

[1] *Canticle of Canticles*, v, 17.
[2] *Canticle*, v, 6.

than this silence. It provides a fitting commentary upon the text which contained the Child's reply : "Did you not know that I must be about my Father's business ?" It is evident that the hidden life, which Jesus again took up, was as much the plan of God as was the flashing revelation of Him for a moment in the Temple.

How is this mysterious period in the life of Jesus to be interpreted ? The deeper side of it, the one that is turned in loving adoration towards His heavenly Father, has just been mentioned. But there is that other side of it, in which Jesus turns in love towards men. Jesus could not, in truth, so give Himself to God without giving Himself to man since man has become, in the daring phrase of Saint Thomas of Aquin, the God of God. Is not the happiness of man the aim of God ? We must see in the perfect way that Jesus expresses human littleness a preparation for His ministry amongst men. The word " preparation " must not be misunderstood. The problem of vocation in life, so difficult for others, was no problem for Jesus. From the first moment of His life in time He was conscious of Himself, He knew His destiny, and He awaited the Father's hour which was, in fact, the hour suited to man's capacities. Jesus will not appear before men as the Messiah until He has the visible authority of mature manhood.

The words with which Saint Luke describes this period of preparation also need a commentary : "And Jesus advanced in wisdom, and age, and grace before God and man." There is a sense in which Jesus could not advance in wisdom or in grace. From the very first He enjoyed the beatific vision with all the gifts of the Spirit in their fullness. But there is also a sense in which He grew in years and advanced in knowledge that came to Him through His human faculties. The knowledge which already He possessed extended, so to speak, to new objects by the use of His senses and His faculties, senses and faculties that really developed in Him by use. He did not, as it were, receive new knowledge but He acquired in a new, an experimental, manner confirmation of knowledge which already He possessed. So fully did Jesus accept the

human nature which He assumed that He was content to grow
from tenderest infancy like any other child. And He
completely wins us by the way in which He ensured this
gradual growth with all its fascination of first smiles and
words and the typical gestures of a childhood that is humble.
He would be in all things, sin excepted, like unto a Son of Man.

Apocryphal Gospels have surrounded the childhood of
Jesus with all kinds of miracles and prodigies. For us, and
the silence of the Gospel is encouraging, the miracle of Jesus
is the naturalness of His childhood. One can see Him as a
very little child in the tender arms of Mary, like any other
child, and see them gaze into each other's eyes for hours
without the flicker of an eyelid. What passes between Child
and Mother in such hours no one can tell. One can see
Him learning, with His first attempts at walking, the words
that Mary teaches Him. In the distance the silent figure of
Saint Joseph awaits Him and bravely the little Child traverses
the distance, or turns back perhaps half-way to find the
protecting arms of His Mother. The Evangelists have not
described such charming scenes but it is lawful to think that
they had their place in the home of Nazareth.

With what truth Jesus will later say : " Take up my yoke
upon you, and learn of me, because I am meek, and humble of
heart : and you shall find rest to your souls." His knowledge
of humility is very real. He Who was God accepts the
humblest conditions of manhood. Just as man, in pride,
would be " like to God " so Jesus, in humility, would be
" like to man." So perfectly does He achieve His purpose
that, except by a certain perfection and a mysterious something that marks him off, He becomes indistinguishable
from the companions of His day. Were not His cousins
scandalised when he began to preach ? Did not Nazareth
itself reject Him ? The humility of Jesus becomes a
stumbling-block to the proud. To this very day it is the same.
The condition of any intimacy with Jesus is humility.

The immediate fruit of the humility of Jesus, nourished
as it was by love, was a super-human patience. When one

remembers the fire that burned in His heart, the flames of love that ascended to the eternal Father to whom, by right, all things belong, one appreciates the significance of patience that submits to the slow-footed hours and days and years. But life is not merely action ; it is inaction. Life is not merely doing ; it is suffering. Life is not merely an occasion for doing great things ; it is also an occasion for being content with one's inability to do anything for God. Jesus has come, in truth, to preach a doctrine, to lay down His life, to give an example. Death will come ; the hour for preaching has not struck ; but it is always time for example. He Who had created time to be the medium in which human life unfolds itself was then content to suffer time in every sense as He waited, in subjection to human parents, for the predestined moment.

Saint Luke does not omit to add : "And he went down with them, and came to Nazareth, and was subject to them." [1] He Who was God was subject, obedient, to Mary and Joseph and out of this subjection was built the ideal home, the ideal society, which is Nazareth. Nazareth is home, the ideal that is unforgettable even in an age which has forgotten many Christian things. One might have gone there of an evening, knocked at the humble door, and be greeted by a Child from whose countenance the light of heaven emanated. He would have admitted you to a heaven upon earth in the form of a holy Trinity : the man, the woman, and the child. The man has been called " just " by holy Scripture ; the woman is she who is " blessed among woman " ; the Child is Saviour of the world. Once to have visited Nazareth, in faith and charity, is to have found new reverence for every home : for the man, who is God's provider ; for the woman, who is the source of life ; for the child who is the saviour of a dying race.

Nazareth is home. It might be any home because it is the ideal of every Christian home. To forget it would be fatal. All must return to it : the proud, to learn humility ; the rich, to contemn their wealth ; the selfish, to learn selflessness ; the worldly, to know what heaven is like ; the

[1] Luke, ii, 51.

poor, to sweeten their poverty ; the worker, to dignify his
labour ; the neglected, to sanctify their obscurity. There is
much to learn.

IV.

Nazareth was a preparation. Hidden away amongst the
hills of Galilee, working and praying and leading a life that
was a challenge to all worldly values, Jesus awaited the hour
of His manifestation. Before Him lay a mighty task. Since
man first broke with God, and tasted death, the empire of
evil had spread its darkness. Satan exercised his way, like a
powerful prince, and filled the minds of men with designs of
evil. In that world of darkness and corruption Nazareth was
the home of light. From Nazareth salvation would go forth
in the Person of Jesus.

For this manifestation of our Lord the way was already
being prepared. After centuries of silence the voice of
prophecy was again heard in Israel. John the Baptist had
begun to preach the advent of the Messiah. This was the son
of Elizabeth, a child of benediction, who knew of Jesus : first,
from the lips of his mother who told him of the signs that
surrounded his birth ; second, from the inner promptings of
the Holy Spirit. Nothing is known of him until he appears, a
weird and striking figure, coming from the desert to which,
as it were, he naturally belongs. His preaching fired the
imagination of the crowd. One had only to look at him to
know that he was a seer, a prophet, and when he spoke of the
Messiah it was as if he beheld the object preaching. " Do
penance," he said, " for the kingdom of heaven is at hand ;
the Lord approaches." Just as Israel was losing hope, the
Baptist declared : "And all flesh shall see the salvation of
God."

The substance of the Baptist's preaching was in two
things : first, an irresistible awakening of the sense of sin and
the need of penance ; second a rite accompanied by confession
which suggested a purification by baptism of water. Both
were preached by him as a prelude, a preparation, and he

declared himself to be a Voice and nothing more. The real significance of his preaching was a reference, growing ever more emphatic, to One greater than he was. One, the latchet of whose shoe he was unworthy to loose. As this reference awakened the curiosity of the people, the question was addressed to him, constantly: " Where is He ? " Avidly the Baptist's eyes would scan, day by day, the throngs of people that came to him. He knows, by a divine instinct, that the Messiah was near. An inner voice told him : " He upon whom thou shalt see the Spirit descending, and remaining upon him, he it is that baptiseth with the Holy Ghost,"[1] And then it happened. Amongst the crowd there stood the sinless, the innocent Lamb of God, a Man amongst men, the Son of Man who now mingled with the throngs that surrounded John. As yet the Baptist did not know Him. Jesus drew near. A sudden vision revealed Him to the Baptist. Over the Head of Jesus the heavens opened and the Spirit, in the form of a dove, descended and rested, *remained*, upon Him. It was the sign for which the Baptist waited. Before him stood the Saviour, humble, ready to go down into the waters of the Jordan. The Baptist protested : " I ought to be baptised by thee, and comest thou to me ? " But Jesus answered gently: " Suffer it to be so now. For so it becometh us to fulfill all justice." The Baptist had further evidence that he was not mistaken. This was the word of perfect Wisdom with which the Son of Man, associating John with Himself as the Voice which proclaims the Word, began to lay the real foundations of justice in a true relation of man to God. Humility is truth and, in particular, the truth of man's relation to God. That Jesus should, in the sight of men, appear a sinner ; that Jesus should receive from John this baptism ; that to the abasement of His hidden life He should add this subjection in the eyes of men : all this is so calculated to overthrow the pride of man, from which flows all human sinfulness, that we cannot fail to recognise that we are in the presence of the Perfect.

Jesus was fully aware of His mission. Justice demanded that the rights of God should be vindicated. It was by this

[1] John, i, 33.

wondrous act of humility that Jesus began to vindicate them. Scarcely had He emerged from the waters of the Jordan when, praying apart, the vision of the open heaven came to Him : "And Jesus being baptized, forthwith came out of the water : and lo, the heavens were opened to him : and he saw the Spirit of God descending as a dove, and coming upon Him. And behold a voice from heaven saying : This is my beloved Son, in whom I am well pleased." [1] He could now inaugurate His public life. The Spirit by whose power He had become Man, the Spirit Whose gifts filled His human soul, the invisible Spirit Who prompted His every thought, desire and action was now revealed as the living Inspiration of all His ways. What is said of that prompting which led Him to the desert might stand as the secret inspiration of His entire life on earth. " Then Jesus was led by the spirit into the desert . . . " The Son of Man Whose motto was the Will of God in all things could only be entirely docile to the Spirit Who is the very Love of God in Person.

[1] Matt., iii, 16, 17.

IV.

Desert.

I.

When it is said that contemplating the Word Incarnate is the source of authentic holiness, it is implied that for life, in all its forms, our blessed Lord is the supreme exemplar of perfection. Life has many forms and it is customary to distinguish between the active and contemplative lives in terms of the predominance of contemplation or action. Saint Thomas, whose teaching on the matter is classical, points out that, in every hypothesis, primacy goes to contemplation of which the active life ideally is the outcome and extension. "But since certain men are especially intent on the contemplation of truth, while others are especially intent on external actions, it follows that man's life is fittingly divided into active and contemplative." [1] At the source of a life, however, in which religion has its rightful place, it will be found that there is a love of charity and charity, of its nature, inclines a man towards contemplation. Who, knowing and loving God, would not want to increase his intimacy with Him ? To begin on earth, however imperfectly, the life of heaven is the aim of the contemplative.

It is characteristic of the modern outlook, dominated as it is by the ideal of action, that it regards the mysterious period of the Master's sojourn in the desert as the immediate preparation for His public ministry. And it is not difficult to find in this period a number of things that have significance for His life of action. But it is not impossible also to find in this period an example of the purely contemplative life with its proper lessons for the contemplatives of every age. It is

[1] *Summa*, IIa IIae., Q.179, a.1.

just the greatness of our blessed Lord Who intends to be the universal Prototype that, in His existence on earth, He gives an example that will have significance for every form that life will assume in the life-story of His Church on earth.

It is true that the Evangelists do not tell us anything of the contemplation of Jesus Himself in the desert. As in other instances where there is reference to the prayer of Jesus, they are content to indicate the external settings of it. "And immediately the Spirit drove Him out into the desert. And he was in the desert forty days and forty nights, and was tempted by Satan : and he was with beasts, and the angels ministered to him." [1] Such is the brief account which Saint Mark has given of the episode. We are left to infer that since the Spirit had descended, and remained upon Him, Jesus seeks the desert by an impulse of the Holy Spirit. Tradition seems to point to a mountain to the west of Jericho, rising up out of an arid and scorched desert-place, as the scene of His sojourn. But Saint Mark himself, in a pithy phrase, gives us an exact picture of its desolation. "And he was with beasts," remarks this Evangelist, suggesting the entire absence of human society. This is true of the contemplative life where, even when contemplatives live together, the cell is regarded as the ideal desert in which to live with God, and with God alone. For it is only when the energies of the mind, which seek an outlet in human commerce, are gathered together in recollection that the contemplative may hope to find the God of his heart. " Behold I will allure her," says the Prophet Osee " and will lead her into the wilderness ; and I will speak to her heart."

Saint Matthew and Saint Luke add a further note to a description not difficult to complete. They say that it is a period of uninterrupted fast : "And he ate nothing in those days ; and when they were ended he was hungry." [2] There is nothing in the public life of Jesus that is like to this, though on occasion He does refer to fasting, [3] and we must see in it the promptings of the Holy Spirit Who helps Him to find

[1] Mark, I, 12–13.
[2] Luke, iv, 2.
[3] Matt., vi, 16–18 and ix, 15.

in the Will of God the nourishment of His life. But it is at least significant that diabolical temptations are associated with the rigorous fast of the desert. May it not be that contemplatives who, by the grace of their vocation, overcome the lower needs of human nature are subject to the attacks of Satan ? Certain it is that souls who draw near to God, who are associated intimately with the Saviour of mankind, are the peculiar objects of Satan's envy. But they have this assurance that, fighting against the enemy of mankind, they are fighting a battle already won. The Evangelists tell us explicitly that Jesus was led by the Spirit into the desert in order to encounter, and defeat, the Prince of darkness. That is why this period of special significance for the contemplative, has its lessons for every Christian engaged in the warfare of life. " Then Jesus was led by the spirit," says Saint Matthew, " to be tempted by the devil." [1]

Saint Paul sheds true light on the tempting of Jesus in a single phrase. " For we have not a high priest." he says, " who can not have compassion on our infirmities : but one tempted in all things like as we are, without sin." [2] The same sentiment finds expression in another place. " For in that, wherein he himself hath suffered and been tempted, he is able to succour them also that are tempted." [3] Granted that certain differences exist between the tempting of Jesus, in Whom there was inner harmony, and that of Christians in whom native weakness conspires with enemies from without, the fact remains that Jesus was tempted and that the temptations, as Saint Bonaventure points out, are precisely those by which man, in the first instance, was overcome. In our blessed Lord's temptations we may see, in fact, the story of all man's tempting and if it be borne in mind, as the Gospel seems to suggest, that it is precisely as Man that Jesus conquered, then we may see in the three temptations the obstacles to be overcome by those who would draw near to the ideal of Jesus Christ the Son of Man in Whom dwelt the Spirit of God in all His fulness. The Master did not yield, He

[1] Matt., iv, 1.
[2] Hebr., iv, 15.
[3] Hebr., ii 18.

defeated Satan as a Man, He proved Himself to be Mary's Offspring Who would crush the Serpent's head, and His victory is a signal one from which Satan, baffled, must have withdrawn in entire confusion. Was it that Jesus, refusing to reveal His Godhead, wished also to shield His Mother ? It is not for us to say. But we cannot ignore the fact that, conquering Satan as Man, with such weapons as grace puts within the reach of every Christian, Jesus shows His anxiety to share with us our infirmity and teach us an enduring lesson upon the nature and kinds of possible temptation and the powers of Satan.

II.

The order in which the temptations are recorded by the Evangelists is not exactly the same in all. That is of little importance. If we consider the three temptations, one by one, we cannot fail to see how intimately related they are to the life of man. Man is a self, a human person, and this self unifies in a marvellous way the natures of living beings as they are found beneath him. Man is a unity, it is true, but he is a complex unity. In man there is a union of spirit and matter and so intimate is that union that the human soul, of its nature spiritual, is the informing principle which contains within it vegetative, animal, and rational life. Such a being, man, is open to temptation on every side : from within, from without, and actually from above in diabolical intervention. Since man first rebelled against God, and lost the higher life of grace by which he was united to God, and in which he had the source of harmony and peace within him, he has become a city whose history is one of revolt, disharmony, and anarchy. Anarchic forces within him conspire with enemies from without and it is as if every nature of which man is compounded desires its own autonomy. Temptation, as a consequence, takes many forms but at the deep source of man is selfhood. Self may identify itself successively with one or other of man's partial natures ; self claims complete autonomy and wants to be a law unto itself ; and the triple temptation unfolds itself as a reflection of what our Lord for our benefit, allowed Himself to suffer.

Saint Paul's observation of man's susceptibility to temptation is penetrating. He describes it as having its source in a perennial conflict, from which no man is entirely immune, between " the flesh " and " the spirit." It would be a mistake to limit this conflict, in accordance with modern usuage, to any one manifestation of " the flesh." The point is that, for Saint Paul, " the flesh" includes the three kinds of temptation with which we are now concerned. " Now the works of the flesh are manifest, which are fornication, uncleanness, immodesty, luxury, idolatory, witchcrafts, enmities, contentions, emulations, wraths . . . and such like." [1] In a word, Saint Paul is thinking of all unrightful claims of a human self which would dispute the rights of God.

A casual glance at the first temptation of our Lord suffices to show the vast extent of its significance. Having fasted forty days and forty nights He experienced hunger. Hunger was the cry of His Body, and in particular of the vegetative life of the body, for a nourishment withheld at the behest of the Father, prompted by the Holy Spirit. Note how the temptation was worded by Satan : " If thou be the Son of God, command that these stones be made bread." The reference of this temptation is clearly indicated : it points to the very source of physical life, the sustenance on which the vegetative life in man depends. But since life in man is nourished by things external to him, it is possible to see in this temptation a symbol of all that, coming from without, appeals to the life of sense. It is true that the very basis of life is nourishment, and that the life of merely sentient beings is, strictly speaking, not capable of excess in the sense in which excess would be a moral fault, still man is not merely a sentient being but rational and spiritual as well. For that reason he is bound to find a true subordination of this part of his complex nature, which craves for pleasure, to the higher ends of the spirit. This temptation may arise for man from many sources, and in various forms, but if the desires aroused are inimical to the ife of the spirit, renunciation is indicated. No better reply to all such temptings can be found than that which is contained in our Saviour's words : " Not in bread alone doth man live ;

[1] Gal., v, 19–21.

but in every word that proceedeth from the mouth of God." [1]
That is the perfect reply.   For the natural man there is a law of
life, which is made known in conscience and verified in the
Commandments ;   for the Christian man the living Law is
Jesus Whose Spirit not only reveals the exigencies of true
perfection but actually empowers a man to overcome the
turbulent desires of his lowest nature.   In truth, it is Jesus
Who, by His Spirit, extends into the present time the
influence of His triumph over Satan who is quick to attack
man at his most vulnerable point.   Is it not significant that,
in the beginning Satan began his attack on woman and opened
it with an appeal to the fruit that was good to look at ?   But if
Eve failed, forgetting as she did the rights of God, Jesus
triumphed in His appeal to God Who is the very Source of
life for man.

III.

The second temptation is an advance upon the first.   This
is how Saint Matthew relates it :   " Then the devil took him up
into the holy city, and set him upon the pinnacle of the
temple.   And said to him : If thou be the Son of God, cast
thyself down . . . "   This temptation, in which Satan so clearly
suggests the destruction towards which he impels humanity, is
best understood when related to man's social nature which is
not unrelated to the animal life that he possesses.   Man is
social by his nature and his dependence on others may be
employed by Satan for his own ends.   A distinction is
sometimes made between pride and vanity, pride being
connected with self-sufficiency and vanity with undue
dependence on the estimate of others.   But it must not be
forgotten that vanity, in its desire to make up for its own
inherent absence of value by a value coming from the opinion
of others, has its roots in pride.   Satan's invitation to our
Lord to make an impressive beginning, in the sight of the
multitudes, by this casting of Himself from the pinnacle of
the Temple is a direct appeal to vain-glory.   The temptation
is not without its subtlety.   He wants to know if our Lord is
really the Son of God, the Messiah, and he quotes for his own
purpose a messianic psalm.   " For it is written : that he hath

[1] Matt. iv, 4.

given his angels charge over thee, and in their hands shall they bear thee up, lest perhaps thou dash thy foot against a stone." [1]   Already foiled in the first temptation, Satan quotes the Scriptures and insidiously pays the Master the compliment of regarding Him as the Messiah.   On the strength of this Satan hopes for an ostentatious showing of Himself to the people.   But he could not hide his own desire that the leap from the pinnacle would be to the Master's destruction.

The reply of our blessed Lord, however, is enigmatic. " It is written again : Thou shalt not tempt the Lord thy God." Satan is non-plussed.   The dictum could mean just what it says : " Thou shalt not tempt Me, the Lord " ; or it could mean that it was not lawful, by presumption, to tempt the Lord, thy God.   Satan could not decide.   But the temptation itself is no casual one : it is calculated to appeal to man's social nature.   Once the lowest nature, as in the first temptation, is overcome, there is just the danger that a man is so exalted that he does not take ordinary precautions and expects Providence to step in with a miracle of preservation. Such a temptation could have no appeal to the Son of Man Who, in the waters of the Jordan, had appeared a Man amongst men whose one ambition was to realise that justice in which man takes up his true position in regard to God.

There is, however, a third temptation which takes us to the roots of the other two.   This is the temptation which had transformed Satan himself and made of him the Prince of darkness.   It is a temptation which follows every man who, having overcome the concupiscence of the flesh and the concupiscence of the eyes, is still faced with the pride of life.   It is extraordinary to what lengths the human self will go to fashion the kingdoms of the world to its own ideas and desires.   Satan leads the Master this time to a height from which the kingdoms of the earth can be discerned.   "All these will I give thee, if falling down thou wilt adore me."   The pride of Satan in this instance is unmistakeable : he is asking for nothing less than adoration.   The prize offered is kingship of the world ; the cost is adoration of evil.   There

[1] Matt. iv, 6.

is something as deep and subtle here as Satan's own darkness. When he does not actually try to convince men of his non-existence, in a pride unconscious of itself, he prompts a man to adore him in many ways : first, by suggesting that man is above the distinction of good and evil ; secondly, by suggesting that evil may be done that good may be realised : thirdly, by an inordinate desire for quick and violent reform which takes no account of God. One is reminded of the desire of two disciples that fire should descend upon the town in Samaria which had closed its gates against them ; or better still, of the taunting cry with which men tempted Jesus to descend from His Cross on Calvary. But all these appeals had no power over Jesus Who knew of what Spirit He was and Who realised that it is the good, not evil, which must triumph. " Begone, Satan ! For it is written : The Lord thy God shalt thou adore, and him only shalt thou serve." [1] Our lord does not argue with the Tempter. He simply takes the sword of the Spirit, the Word of God, and vindicates successively, the inalienable rights of God. " Then the devil left him ; and behold angels came and ministered to him." [2]

After the temptations, the Gospel says, Satan retired from Him for a time. But Satan was at work. In vain, however, were Satan's machinations. To overcome him Jesus, accepting fully the conditions of His Manhood, made the Will of God, the rights of God, the weapon of Satan's defeat. And when the enemies of Christ, inspired no doubt by Satan, cried out, " If thou be the Son of God, come down from the Cross," the taunt fell harmless at the Feet of Him Who freely bound Himself to the Cross of Calvary. From death Jesus would rise again, by the Spirit of God, to continue down the ages in the frail bodies of mortal men and women His enduring triumph over the enemy of mankind "Wherefore as by one man sin entered into this world, and by sin death ; and so death passed upon all men, in whom all have sinned . . . Therefore, as by the offence of one, unto all men to condemnation ; so also by the justice of one, unto all men to justification of life." [3]

[1] Matt., iv, 10.
[2] Matt., iv, 11.
[3] Roms., v, 12–18.

V.

Happiness

The life of our blessed Lord is mirrored in certain words
that have an almost magical power of evocation. Bethlehem
signifies the gentle dawn ; Nazareth weaves around Him
veils of mystery ; Jerusalem is the scene of dramatic conflict.
But His public life may be said to unfold itself beneath the
open sky, around the Lake in Galilee. Less impressive
perhaps than Jerusalem, with its hallowed associations,
Genesareth is more touching in its appeal. Like a magnet
it draws to itself the mind and we find our thoughts, like
homing birds, poised above its quiet depths. It was here
that Jesus spoke ; the echoes of His voice have never died ;
the Lake is a centre whose circumference cannot be traced.

In the days of our Lord's earthly ministry Genesareth
was a busy centre. Its banks were studded over with a dozen
villages whose names are still familiar. Jesus must have often
passed from one side of it to the other, crossing the Lake to
reach Capharnaum, regarded by many as His home, or going
on foot to Bethsaida, Chorozain or Magdala. The modern
traveller, it is said, is disappointed. What was once a centre
of busy activity is now desolate and abandoned. A solitary
boat may lie lonely upon its waters ; a few nomadic tents
are visible on its banks ; silence reigns upon the scene. But
a man should be very insensitive to atmosphere, and
unimaginative, to whom that silence would not offer, once
again, the words of Jesus.

Surrounded on every side by little mounts and plateaux,
the Lake still guards within its depths faint echoes of that
deathless Voice. Such power had the voice of Jesus in life

that men were enticed away, by the music of it, from the cities of their cares and from the body's imperious needs of thirst and hunger. Echoes of that living Voice are not less powerful. Any man who knows himself the contemporary of Jesus will find, as they come to life within him, that he is awakened, like the Jews of old, to spiritual aspirations of which he has but a fitful vision. It was here amidst the hills of Galilee, around the quiet Lake, that heaven was lowered to earth as Jesus spoke the eternal gospel of human happiness.

Saint Matthew reports the incident we have in mind. He sets himself, as also does Saint Luke, to be as impressive as the chaste style of an Evangelist will allow. A crowd of people has gathered ; disciples surround the Master : Jesus is seated upon a rock. "And seeing the multitudes, he went into a mountain, and when he was set down, his disciples came unto him. And opening his mouth, he taught them . . . "[1] Every word of that description is deliberate. No better introduction could be found to suggest the expectant silence of the multitude. And the introduction was intended as a prelude to the most momentous Sermon ever preached. Scholars have exercised their ingenuity to decide whether this Sermon represents a single discourse or whether it is not an epitome of other sermons. It is not unlikely that it is, in fact, one single sermon. But it matters little. The important thing is that Jesus spoke it, Jesus Who was God as well as man, and that His words addressed to the little Galilean congregation were intended for the world at large.

The Sermon on the Mount, so compact in the richness of its inner unity, bears upon it the stamp of a creative Genius as far as possible exalted above the simple minds of the men who recorded it. The vast significance of this Sermon, of its every living phrase, is literally inexhaustible ; it is a contribution to the world's literature whose source is more than human. Men of genius, like Saint Augustine and Saint Thomas of Aquin, pondered over it until their minds, enriched by the truth of it, composed vast treatises that are the wonder of succeeding eyes. Nor is it possible to doubt

[1] Matt., v, 1-2.

the continuity of their teaching with the rich simplicity of the Gospel. Aquinas made no mistake when he said this Sermon contains within its scope the entire perfection of the Christian way of life ; [1] for that precisely is what the Sermon is—an epitome of wisdom from on High. The Sermon is, in fact, the very centre of the Master's doctrine, the synthesis of His preaching, Whose efficacy the parable of the Sower was intended to illustrate. And if we look to the effects of a Sermon which ends with a blessing for human suffering, we shall find them gathered into one in the miracle of the Saviour's transfiguration upon another Mount. To put the matter briefly, The Sermon on the Mount contains the Master's doctrine ; the parable of the Sower illustrates its intrinsic efficacy ; in the Transfiguration of Thabor we behold in the Person of Jesus the sublime end to which it leads. Nothing less than a transvaluation of human values, a veritable transformation of human nature, is the purpose aimed at by our blessed Lord in this magnificent gospel of human happiness.

It will not have escaped your notice that the Sermon is a doctrine of happiness. Just as the Gospel itself signifies " good tidings," so this epitome of the Gospel is a doctrine of human bliss or blessedness. Jesus knew what was deepest in the human spirit. So profound in every man is this desire for happiness that its impulse is the very instinct of his life. There is not within the confines of the created universe a being, however humble, in which the urge for its perfection is not operative. But in man where cosmic forces meet, the consciousness of perfection is happiness. For that reason the problem facing every man, the question implicit in all his questions, is precisely the abiding mysery of man's real purpose and destiny. No great teacher has ever found the ear of humanity who has not had some theory of life's ultimate meaning and no man has deeply reflected without finding at the very source of all his thoughts this very impulse towards the achievement of perfection. There is no philosophy, no real account of man and the world in which he lives, which is not, at the same time, an answer to the question of human

[1] In Matt., v.

happiness. This is the true, because the only adequate, approach to the Sermon on the Mount, In a special setting, with full awareness of His mission, Jesus announces, in systematic form, His heavenly teaching on life's real purpose, perfection, and happiness. The better to arouse men's attention to the originality of His doctrine, Jesus has recourse to paradox. It is not difficult to imagine the disturbance of accepted standards created by His utterances. To a people inclined to find in material prosperity a sign of God's predilection He proclaims : " Blessed are the poor in spirit . . ." Who could have thought it ? Who could have realised that to renounce created things, in fact or in desire, is to be enriched with the wealth of Godhead ? He follows up with " Blessed are the meek . . . " in a direct challenge to that will to power which delights to exercise its sway. He piles paradox on paradox until one has the impression of a series of negations, negations that seem to frustrate the very impulse of life itself. But it is just these very negations which, properly understood, are the condition of that " more abundant " life which Jesus said He had come on earth to impart.

From beginning to end the Sermon on the Mount unfolds itself in a series of striking paradoxes. But mark you well. To imagine, as some have done, that the doctrine is merely negative, or that Jesus was thinking only of a blessedness deferred, is to miss the point. In each of the Beatitudes there are, remarks Saint Thomas, two things : first, the merit, as in " Blessed are the poor in spirit " ; secondly, the reward, as in " for theirs is the kingdom of heaven." But this reward is not limited to eternity ; it finds its place in time. It may happen, for instance, that the good may be deprived of material rewards but not, even in this life, of a spiritual recompense which initiates the true beatitude.[1] Jesus knew that the greatest paradox of all, His own death, could make effective His exhortations. His vision took in the unborn future. He would merit for humanity the infusion of the self-same Spirit by which He lived. In the strength of the Spirit men would be capable of superhuman perfection. Jesus therefore set no limit to the heroism He asked for, just as there was no limit

[1] In Matt., V.

to the blessedness He promised. His ultimate exhortation was the magnificent injunction : " Be you therefore perfect . . . " [1] So convinced was Saint Thomas of the integrity of the Sermon's content that he did not hesitate to write : " Just as Moses, legislating for man, added other things which are reducible to the Commandments, so Christ in His teaching gave Beatitudes to which all things else are reducible." [2] In the Sermon on the Mount there is finality, a veritable completeness, of doctrine.

II.

Never had the ideal of happiness, or the doctrine of it, found expression in accents so magnificent and arresting. Other systems emanating from merely human genius, however noble, do not stand comparison with the ideal as Jesus saw it. For Him the happiness for which man is destined is something more than human : it is nothing less than a sharing in the bliss of Godhead. So transcendent is this ideal that to reach it man must be made anew, regenerated, so as to find within him an added life, a sharing in God's own nature, which will make it possible for man to reach a destiny beyond his natural powers. Unless this is appreciated there is no understanding of the Sermon on the Mount.

Any doctrine of life or happiness, in fact, must begin here because the first thing to be decided is the ultimate end or purpose for which man exists. Man is a thing unfinished. Deep in his being is desire, and desire is born of that affinity which obtains between a thing imperfect and the fullest realisation of its nature. " The end of all things," says St. Thomas, " is their perfection." Now man is what he is by his capacity for thought. That is why, unlike the animal, he is perplexed by the problem of his destiny. It would not be too much to say that all great systems of human happiness fall into one or other of three great groups according as men have identified the supreme good for life with pleasure, utility, or with a perfection befitting man's rational nature. In these three accounts it is not difficult to note an ascending hierarchy

[2] Matt., v. 48.
[3] In Matt., V.

of values. But a perfection befitting man's rational nature
may be of two kinds : the one, proportionate to human nature
and achieved by man's natural powers ; the other, out of all
proportion to man's natural powers and yet mysteriously
adapted to the capacities of the human spirit. The first
is· that natural perfection of which pagan philosophers, and
those whose minds are unenlightened by Faith, have spoken ;
the other is the supernatural, divine, perfection envisaged in
the Beatitudes.

To assure ourselves on this important point we have
only to direct our attention to that Beatitude which, like a
focus of light, illumines all the others : " Blessed are the
pure of heart for they shall see God." Discussing this
Beatitude Saint Thomas refers to the views of those for whom
a vision of God face to face is excluded as impossible. He
replies in the name of reason and of faith : in the name of
reason, because of that capacity which he finds in human
nature to be elevated to a higher supernatural end ; in the
name of faith, since sacred Scripture explicitly affirms the
contrary. " We know," says Saint John, " that when he
shall appear we shall be like to him because we shall see him
as he is." [1] Saint Paul is no less emphatic : " We see now
through a glass in a dark manner ; but then face to face.
Now I know in part ; but then I shall know even as I am
known." [2] It was precisely to call men to this vision of God
face to face, and to make it possible, that Jesus came on earth.

This possibility, however, can become effective only in
the renovation of human nature by the gift of sanctifying
grace. The reason is not difficult to grasp. The happiness
in store for man is the vision of God face to face. But such a
destiny is beyond the natural powers of man to reach. No
being, in fact, could naturally behold God save God Himself.
It follows that we must receive that participation in the divine
Nature which is grace. And this must take place here and
now if there is to be any real proportion between human
action and human destiny. If heaven is to be merited, if
man is to enter into everlasting life, he must be " re-born,"

[1] 1 John, iii, 2.
[2] 1 Cor., xiii, 12.

as Jesus said to Nicodemus, so that the new life will be the root and source of supernatural activities. The life of heaven is begun on earth, amidst the shadows and images of the Faith, when man is graced by God, in the happy phrase of Saint Augustine, by the presence of His Spirit within his soul and life. For then, and only then, has the message of the Beatitudes any real meaning for him.

There is continuity between earth and heaven. In each Beatitude is offered a foretaste of eternal bliss. To the poor in spirit happiness is promised because in them has begun the reign of the Spirit and where the Spirit is present, enlightening and empowering, the instinct for progress, with corresponding recompense, is active, But the seeing of God face to face dominates the entire movement of the soul. It would be a mistake to think that the Christian's happiness on earth is equivalent to the perfect bliss of heaven. But it is a very real thing. No saint would exchange the consolations of the Spirit for anything the world prizes most. He is not only certain that joys, whose source in the midst of afflictions could only be the Spirit of Christ, are very real compared with oases seen by other men in the desert of time, but he has the assurance that these very joys are the gentle murmur of that Ocean of joy which is the Godhead. "And sometimes," cried out the great Augustine, " you admit me to a state of mind that I am not ordinarily in, a kind of delight which, could it be made permanent in me, would be hard to distinguish from the life to come . . . "

III.

To have discovered the ideal is to find light for the actual life of man on earth : the ideal is the meaning of the actual. But if man is destined by God, Who made him, for a destiny beyond his reach, man must enter on the way which the light of Faith will teach him. A thing unfinished, eminently capable of perfection, the human being is free : he must be the active agent of his own perfection. Now the most potent means for the achieving of perfection is virtue. There are many kinds of virtue but the fundamental role of virtue, as a quality of action, is the forming and the fashioning of a certain kind of character, natural in the unregenerate, and Christian in the follower of Christ. One isolated action does not constitute virtue. What is needed is a permanent disposition of personality, a kind of second nature, which will express itself in action at once free and facile, prompt and joyous and consistent. Until a man is in this way rescued from the incoherent play of mood and passion, and takes on the firm texture of character, no ideal can shed steady illumination on his attempts at living.

That man is capable of the perfection which virtue adds to his native, unformed being, is clear from an inspection of his structure. Endowed with reason, he is able to organise his conduct by the interplay of ends and means ; in every sphere he shows that he is capable of habits that economise his energy and increase his powers ; life in him makes sure that, whether he will or no, the place of habit shall be recognised. But before the prospect of a supernatural ideal man is powerless. To remedy this native insufficiency God provides him with virtues, which are infused, so that man may be as well equipped in the supernatural, as he is in the natural, order. Faith itself is such a virtue. Without it, the Beatitudes themselves would have little or no meaning. Now Faith is a beginning. Other virtues come with grace, they are infused, and they are intended to help the life of grace to penetrate the natural life and spread its light throughout the vast range of human conduct. Towards the highest summits of holiness on earth, and the fullest measure of human perfection, the Beatitudes point the way.

Man, in grace, does not cease to be himself. Deep at the source of his actions, and manifested by them, the love of man's being for its perfection is at work. In various ways does this love find expression : the kind of ideal that appeals to him shows the kind of a man he is. That is why, in theory as well as in practice, happiness has been sought from pleasure, or from utility, or from the perfection which befits man's rational nature. There are many reasons for this division of opinion. But the complexity of human nature itself, wherein disordered inclinations from within conspire with allurements from without, lies at the immediate source of it : man may identify himself with one or other of the natures gathered into one within him ; he may even strive to find a perfection in defiance of God's designs. On last analysis the great option is to find happiness in God or in Self, and Saint Augustine summed up the choice when he said that the City of God is built by the cult of God even to the contempt of self, whereas the earthly City has its source in the cult of self even to the contempt of God. Now the earthly City, for which Scripture has found the term " world," is ruled by three great forces which can wreck the happiness of man. " For all that is in the world," said Saint John, " is the concupiscence of the flesh, and the concupiescence of the eyes, and the pride of life, which is not of the Father, but is of the world." [1] It follows that the very first condition of a life of virtue is the renunciation of the Self : not in Self must man seek happiness. This will mean a combat and a victory, for renunciation of the Self, as the goal of one's existence, is a gain and not a loss. But until this victory is won, Self will obtrude its claims at once directly and indirectly : directly, when a man knowingly refuses to accept the law and provision of God ; indirectly, when he seeks his happiness in pleasure which panders to his lowest nature or in those other social substitutes for happiness which are praise or honour, success or renown. To ensure his success he needs a love that will rescue him from the dominance of Self, and God provides him with the virtue of charity which enables his will to exercise a love which is the effective realisation of what Faith has begun in him. Not every kind of love is charity. Charity is of God and, at the very least, it requires a disposition to give God His rightful place as the first Object of human love ; this is a strict minimum. But grace must increase its power over human life, and charity must grow, for perfection is to be sought particularly in charity : "But above all these things have charity, which is the bond of perfection." [2]

There are degrees, however, of charity. Perfection is not the work of a day or of an hour. The width and extent,

[1] 1 John, ii, 16.
[2] Col., iii, 14.

the height and depth of charity in the heart of man finds singular illumination from the Master's teaching in the Beatitudes. In no other part of the Gospels perhaps is the real opposition between the wisdom of the children of God and the wisdom of the world so systematically expounded as here. The spirit of the world employs the three concupiscences for its purpose and the man who submits to them tastes bitterness and death. The Beatitudes are an emphatic challenge, made impressive by their paradoxes, on the part of our blessed Lord. The aim of virtue, said Saint Thomas, is : first, to remove from man the evil which fascinates his heart ; second, to establish him firmly in the exercise of all that is good and noble ; third, to impart to his life the splendour of a certain excellence to be found in works of genius. These objectives are precisely the ideals envisaged by our blessed Lord in the programme of the Beatitudes. Not only do they, when fully accepted, cut off the sources of evil which are the great concupiscences, and set man down in the way of action at once noble and befitting, but they bring with them an aspiration, and the living Source of perfection, by which a man is led towards the heights of heroism.

An ascending order can therefore be discerned in the Sermon on the Mount. In the early Beatitudes a happiness is promised which can be experienced only in a turning away from sin and in an emancipation from all that could impede the flight of the soul to God : there is poverty of spirit, meekness of heart, and the tears of penance. Then follow two Beatitudes that are primarily concerned with the life of action : hunger and thirst for justice direct the soul towards God ; and mercy ensures a perfect attitude towards others. The last two Beatitudes belong, properly, to the life of con-templation : purity of heart, which disposes a man to see God ; and peace, which flows into his soul from wisdom. Finally, there is a crowning Beatitude, the one that summarises them all, in the impressive words of Jesus : " Blessed are they that suffer persecution for justice sake : for theirs is the kingdom of heaven." [1]

[1] Matt., v, 10.

How men could ignore the sublimity of this fragment from the Gospel, in comparison with which any page of mere human literature is dark and dull, is difficult to explain. Perhaps it is that the challenge of its light is too great for the spirit of the world with its standards and its petty measures of success. Men will continue to place their happiness in pleasure and to such as these the poverty which Jesus preached and practised will have little appeal. And it is the same with each of the Beatitudes in turn. But to those who accept our Lord, as He would have Himself accepted, the final Beatitude speaks a special message. Never was such a thing proclaimed before by any man. Not only does Jesus promise a future happiness but He asks them to esteem themselves happy in the midst of tribulations and sufferings : " Blessed are ye when they shall revile you, and persecute you, and speak all that is evil against you, untruly, for my sake. Be glad and rejoice . . . " [1] When He uttered these words, He was thinking of the Cross on which, in poverty, chastity, and obedience He would consecrate His doctrine in His blood and He must have had vision of the many living Images of Himself throughout the ages who would witness to the peace and joy which can inundate the soul in the midst of the most appalling sufferings.

[1] Matt. v 12, 13.

VI.

Eucharist.

I.

Creation is the art of God. Had we but eyes to see, we should behold in a drop of dew upon the frailest flower the glory of His Face. Since first He rescued the trembling light from the abyss of darkness and called to their watches the stars of the night, since first He built this house of creation to be man's abode, there is not a single thing that is not eloquent of its Maker. Whether we view the world in whole or in part, whether our eyes regard its surface as a scene of rest or whether we listen to the throbbing pulse of its incessant activity, the splendour of its order reflects the beauty of God's wisdom : "How great are thy works, O Lord ! Thou hast made all things in wisdom." [1]

The Spirit of wisdom is abroad in God's creation. In other days when men pondered on the works of God, and were enlightened from on high, it seemed to them that wisdom was a living thing : "Doth not wisdom cry aloud, and prudence put forth her voice ? Standing in the top of the highest places by the way, in the midst of the paths, beside the gates of the city, in the very doors she speaketh, saying : "O ye men, to you I call, and my voice is to the sons of men." [2] It is true. We meet wisdom on the roads of life and in the highways ; her dwelling is in the skies and seas ; and when there comes a hush upon all things, the soul being hushed to her very self, we find her in our hearts whispering to us the secret of God's sweetness.

[1] Ps. ciii 24.
[2] Prov. viii, 1–4.

It is just the tragedy of men that, having ears, they will
not listen to the voice of wisdom : " O children, how long
will you love childishness, and fools covet those things
which are hurtful to themselves, and the unwise hate
knowledge ? " [1] Seers of old, dispersed amongst the Gentiles,
exhausted their ingenuity in depicting her charms and in
telling of her high lineage : "Who hath gone up into heaven,
and taken her, and brought her down from the clouds ? Who
hath passed over the sea, and found her, and brought her
preferably to chosen gold ? There is none that is able to
know her ways, nor that can search out her paths." [2] The
truth is that she has " come out from the mouth of the most
High," [3] that "her delights are to be with the children of men." [4]
and that she is not indifferent to the desires of men : " For
wisdom is glorious, and never fadeth away, and is easily
seen by them that love her, and is found by them that seek
her . . . He that awaketh early to seek her shall not labour ;
for he will find her sitting at his door. To think therefore
upon her is perfect understanding." [5]

To people whose religious imaginations were filled with
such poetic visions Jesus spoke in their own terms on one
occasion. To us His words may sound mysterious but to such
a people their meaning should have been clear. He said to
them : " But whereunto shall I esteem this generation to be
like ? It is like to children sitting in the market place.
Who crying to their companions say : we have piped to you,
and you have not danced ; we have lamented, and you have not
mourned. For John came neither eating nor drinking ; and
they say : he hath a devil. The Son of man came eating and
drinking, and they say : behold a man that is a glutton and
a wine drinker, a friend of publicans and sinners. And
wisdom is justified by her children." [6] There is a beautiful
irony in this picture of a people who boasted that they were
the heirs of wisdom. Wisdom had come to them, first, as a

[1] Prov., i, 22.
[2] Baruch iii, 29–31.
[3] Ecclus., xxiv, 5.
[4] Cf. Proverbs, viii, 31.
[5] Wisdom, vi, 13, 15, 16.
[6] Matt. xi, 16–19.

Voice and now as a Word, and they failed to recognise her ; they preferred their unreasonable childishness.

Wisdom is never without her testimony. Wherever wisdom is, there are three things which have power to fascinate: first, the presence of the ideal which is the light of all her ways ; second, the perfect choice of means adapted to the realisation of her ends ; third, the power with which she bends the most unresponsive materials to the magic of her artistry. These are, in effect, the traits of perfect wisdom. If we would really find her, if we would see her in all the ravishing brightness of her God-given beauty we must find that house which was built by wisdom, the house of the seven pillars,[1] wherein Jesus Himself invites us : " Whosoever is a little one, let him come to me. And to the unwise she said : " Come, eat my bread, and drink the wine which I have mingled for you. Forsake childishness, and live, and walk by the ways of prudence." [2]

It is not possible, for long, to think of the Holy Eucharist without a sudden sense of recognition : we are face to face with the masterpiece of God's artistry ; we have found the dwelling-place on earth of Wisdom. When we surrender to it, as surrender we must, we are at a loss which to admire the most : the sublime ideal for man to which it points ; the perfect adaptation of the chosen means ; or the actual transfiguration of humanity beneath its power. There is finality in the Holy Eucharist as a work of God. With surest instinct the Church speaks of it as the marvel of all marvels, the sacrament full of wonder, which concentrates within it the wisdom of the most High God. In breathless admiration she cries out in the words of the Psalmist : " He hath made a remembrance of his wonderful works, being a merciful and gracious Lord : he hath given food to them that fear him." [3]

Wisdom is of God. It is that reality in God which holds together, as in a living sheaf, His other attributes.

[1] Prov. ix, 1.
[2] Prov. ix, 4–6.
[3] Ps. cx, 4.

" For she is the brightness of eternal light and the unspotted mirror of God's majesty, and the image of his goodness." [1] There is knowledge in it, which is the brightness of eternal life, but it is a knowledge transfused by love ; there is power in it, which is the unspotted mirror of God's majesty, but it is omnipotence in the service of love. That is why, in fine, it is the image of God's goodness. God is Love. Hence wisdom in God is a love that reflects and plans ; it is a power that executes the designs of love ; it is above all a goodness without limit whose sole ambition is to share with nothingness the inexhaustible wealth of God's inner Life.

We have only to watch the divine Artist at work to glimpse the splendour of His ideal. Upon the horizon of His thought we can discern man, man for whom He creates the earth and sky, man in whom He recapitulates the work of five mysterious days, man in anticipation of whose advent wisdom sings joyously at her creative task, man who is to be the very " City of thy rest." [2] Do we exalt man too much who have heard that " God created man to his own image ; to the image of God he created him " ? [3] Sharing with him the life of Godhead, making of him an object worthy of divine contemplation, seeing the very splendour of His own Being returning from this final work of creative hands, the divine Artist rested, declaring His work to be exceeding good. [4]

If we are perturbed by the subsequent history of man whose sad prerogative it was to smash the image that God had made, and open the door to death, if with the Psalmist we feel inclined to cry out, " What is man that thou art mindful of him?" [5] then we must think of the patience of God's wisdom which reacheth mightily from end to end of time. Man failed ; but the Ideal remained. There is a mysterious text of Saint Paul which speaks of the first man as " a figure of him who was to come." [6] A figure, of its nature, takes its

[1] Wisdom, vii, 26.
[2] Eccli, xxxvi, 15.
[3] Gen., i, 27.
[4] Gen., i, 31.
[5] Ps., viii, 5.
[6] Rom., v, 14.

meaning from the reality of which it is a figure. Was it that God, in creating men, had before His mind the Ideal Man ? What we do know, for certain, is that Jesus, the Son of Mary, was theWord, the living Image of Godhead in human form, the Man in Whom alone the delight of God could rest. In Jesus humanity was raised to its former greatness, and immeasurably beyond it, and He can share with men the fullness of Life which He possesses. When men accept from Him that Life, when identity with Him is realised by grace, then, and only then, will the Image of God shine forth in splendour from the soul of a renovated humanity.

It is necessary to grasp the import of this which is an invitation to man to seek in himself the blurred image of the ideal for which he was originally created. There is, in fact, a Christian counterpart to the injunction of the mysterious ancient oracle, Know Thyself. Fathers of the Church like Saint Ambrose and Saint Augustine, not to speak of Saint Gregory, have insisted upon it. It is an inspiration common to Saint Bernard and Saint Bonaventure. Saint Bonaventure, for instance, never tires of asking man to consider himself attentively to see : how generously he has been fashioned by nature ; how vilely deformed he has been by sin ; how beautifully reformed he has been by grace.[1] Saint Thomas explains that the image of God may be found in man in a threefold way : first, because man has a natural aptitude for knowing and loving God ; second, because man actually knows and loves God, though in an imperfect manner ; third, in as much as man is able to know and love God in a perfect way.[2] The perfect mode, however, depends upon man's likeness to Jesus, the Son of God, a likeness which can be brought about only by the grace of divine adoption and by man's incorporation with Christ. That this sublime ideal was, in truth, the aim of God becomes inescapably clear from the moment Jesus broaches the question of the Bread of Life.

[1] Sol., Cap. i, No. 1.
[2] 1a. Q., xciii, a. 4.

II.

The effect of the Master's preaching upon the people is illustrated by an incident that took place towards the end of the first period of His ministry in Galilee. The whole province, with the one exception of His native town of Nazareth, had surrendered to Him. There was something about His Person, some hidden attraction, which when He spoke, sufficed to draw men and women to His side. He found it difficult, in fact, to escape from the multitudes. Anxious to give a rest to His disciples, and to prepare them in prayer for struggles yet to come, He took a boat and crossed the sea of Tiberias into a solitary country, called the desert, near the city of Bethzaida.

The attempt was destined to fail. Scarcely had the Master and His disciples landed, than they were followed by a multitude in the neighbourhood of five thousand people. It is true that the people followed because of the miracles he had worked, but it is also evident that they hungered spiritually for the words He uttered. This desert-place was bounded on the north by a mountain with a slight incline towards the plain. It was here that Jesus sat down to instruct the people and to heal the sick that had been brought to Him. The disciples were scattered around the Master; the Feast of the Passover was near at hand.

The Master raised His voice, sending out His words upon the quiet of the desert, and the people experienced the magic of His oratory—calm, compelling and full of beauty. Hours passed unnoticed. They were caught up in the music of His voice and forgot their needs. As the sun went down suddenly, and evening came, they awakened to the fact that it was now too late to return by sea and they had brought no food with them. But the Master had remembered. Seeing the multitudes He had compassion on them.

Amongst the group there was one, an eye-witness, who has kept for us every precious detail of this occasion. Saint John recalls that Jesus turns to His disciples to speak, as it were in private, to them.   He addressed Himself to Philip, Whom He wishes to try, saying : "Whence shall we buy bread that these may eat ? "   Philip is terrified.   Quickly he calculates the cost, knowing the poverty of His Master, and says : " Two hundred pennyworth of bread is not sufficient for them, that every one may take a little . . ."   We are grateful to Philip because, showing the impossibility of feeding this multitude, he guarantees the superhuman character of what actually takes place.   Another disciple then appears : it is Andrew, Simon's brother, He announces that a young boy has brought with him a few barley loaves and two fishes, adding : " But what are these among so many ? "   So does the scene come to life before our eyes.   Saint John adds the little detail that there was much grass in the place.   Jesus makes the people sit down and the few barley loaves are blessed by the Hand of Him Who from a single grain is able to draw a harvest. The people are fed.   The fragments left over are gathered up in many baskets.   And this is His prelude to the mystery of His holy Eucharist.

It is not difficult to imagine the effect of this striking miracle upon the minds of the Galileans.   So impressed were they, so taken with His preaching and His power, that they wished to make Him king.   The Master saw their purpose.   To escape it He retired into the desert and hid from them.   Profiting by the darkness of the night He returned to the sea and, despite a great storm that had arisen, He came to His disciples walking upon the waters.   The disciples were on their way to Capharnaum ; they were twenty-five furlongs from the coast ; it was the fourth watch of the night.   All these details are of Saint John who knew the lake.   They took Him into the boat ; presently they found themselves at the other side ; they went with Him to Capharnuam.

But there was no escape.   The people had returned by the morning and were obstinate in their determination to make Him king.   The multiplication of the loaves had particularly impressed them, because it was a tradition, amongst the Jews, that the Messiah, when He came would, like Moses, give them bread from heaven. Alluding to this tradition, and to the miracle thay had witnessed, they sought confirmation by asking : "What sign dost thou show, that we may see and may believe thee ? . . . Our fathers did eat manna in the desert, as it is written : He gave them bread from heaven to eat." [1]

Seeing how very wrong they were, realising that they wished to fashion Him to the image of their own liking, and convinced that, if He refuses, they will reject Him in the anger of their disappointed hopes, Jesus temporises : He does not at once accept their challenge. He corrects their dictum that it was Moses who gave them bread from heaven and raises their minds to the real Donor, God. He tells them, in fact, that He is Himself the Bread from heaven : " I am the bread of life : he that cometh to me shall not hunger ; and he that believeth in me shall never thirst." [2] That is the immediate introduction : Jesus must be accepted for what He is. The manner of their acceptance must be faith : "Amen, amen I say unto you : he that believeth in me, hath everlasting life." Only when faith has come, opening their minds to the truth of His message, can He accept the challenge of the manna.

It was then, of a sudden, with a change of meaning which is clearly marked, that Jesus makes the promise of the Bread of Life. The transition is as palpable as it was staggering, to their incredulity. No longer was it a question of faith, nor yet of accepting Him for what He is, but something still more mysterious, transcendent, ineffable : " I am the bread of life. Your fathers did eat manna in the desert : and are dead. This is the bread which cometh down from heaven ; that if any man eat of it, he may not die. I am the living bread which came down from heaven. If any man eat of this bread, he shall live for ever : and the bread that I will give is my flesh, for the life of the world." [3] As He uttered these words He saw the darkness of unbelief in their eyes, He saw the gesture of refusal in their souls, but not abating

[1] John, vi, 30.
[2] John vi, 35.
[3] John, vi, 48–52.

one whit He went from affirmation to affirmation, solemnly
inculcating His words at every breath, and ending in a
proclamation which is the very law of life : "Amen, amen,
I say unto you : except you eat the flesh of the Son of man,
and drink His blood, you shall not have life in you. He that
eateth my flesh and drinketh my blood, hath everlasting life :
and I will raise him up in the last day." [1]

The whole incident is characteristic of the Master.
By the magic of His presence He had drawn them out into the
desert, had made them forget their corporeal needs ; He had
offered them the very Bread of Life. When that failed, just
because it was a question of life and death, wisdom asserted
its rights and He had recourse to a solemn command. He does
not stop to explain just how His aim is to be achieved : no
explanation would have altered their incredulity. No
explanation was offered. He meant exactly what He said.
He saw the men who, only a short while before, would have
made him a king turn away from Him in disappointment. He
looked at His disciples, and said : "Will you also go away ? "
And Simon Peter answered him : "Lord, to whom shall we go ?
Thou hast the words of eternal life." Wisdom is justified
in her children.

III.

These words, uttered in the name of the twelve, merited
for the apostles that final scene of intimacy in which the
Master fulfilled His promise. Just as the first stirrings of
the storm that was to break upon Him are heard, when the
sentence of death has already been passed upon Him, Jesus in
His wisdom makes the final preparation for the gift of Life
to men. Under the very shadow of Calvary, with the Cross
looming up before His gaze, He selects the Cenacle in which
to spread His banquet of Life. He has in spirit passed
the portals of death, and now, putting from Him the cares of
the Passion, He proposes to defeat the enemies of God : He
will live for all time upon the earth so that He may nourish

[1] John, vi, 54.

those who accept Him with the Bread of Life and depose within their very bodies the germ of immortality and resurrection.

" Jesus, knowing that his hour was come, that he should pass out of this world to the Father ; having loved his own who were in the world, he loved them unto the end." [1] That is how Saint John introduces the banquet of the Last Supper ; and it is the perfect introduction. It strikes the keynote to all that is to follow. "With desire," said Jesus, " I have desired to eat this Pasch with you." [2] It is a sacred hour, an hour in which He concentrates the sweetness of eternity, an hour in which words of love are heard from the lips of God that will never die in the heart of humanity. No sooner have they celebrated the ancient Pasch, than Jesus inaugurates the new. As we watch the manner of it, our minds flash back to that first gesture with which He had opened His public ministry, a gesture of humility.

Rising from the table, laying aside His cloak, girding His loins with a cloth and taking a vessel of water in His hands, Jesus kneels before them, beginning with Peter. Had we never known it, we should have learned from Jesus that love in truth is humble. Was it that in that moment He was seized, as it were, with a divine respect for these humble men, these simple men whom God had chosen to share in His priesthood ? If He who is the King of angels, the very Son of God, so humbles Himself, what of us ? It is one thing to humble oneself before a superior or an equal, but it is another thing to humble oneself before an inferior. " Believe me." said Saint Bonaventure, " that if a man is really solicitous about being truly humble, he will in this way acquire more grace in a month than another would in forty years." Peter abashed, protests. Jesus insists. He would teach them humility, humility without which Life cannot be received, humility without which purity cannot be preserved : as a man humbles himself so will God exalt him. The feet of His ministers must be cleaned against the dust of the way, for

---

[1] John, xiii, 1.
[2] Luke, xxii, 15.

they who are bearers of Life to others will walk in perilous paths.

Coming back to the table, Jesus explains what He has done and begins that immortal discourse in which He pours out His heart to them in expressions of love, with warnings too, and sometimes with tender reproaches. He comforts them in anticipation of His departure ; He tells them of the mansions that are in His Father's house ; He insists that He will not leave them orphans ; He promises the gift of His Spirit ; He exhorts them to love one another in a new commandment which He gives them. At a definite stage in this discourse, He takes the bread into His hands, gives thanks to God, and breaks it saying : " This is my Body." Taking the Chalice in like manner He says : " This is the chalice, the new testament in my blood, which shall be shed for you." He communicates His apostles.

The effect was instantaneous. Whatever doubts or difficulties they may have entertained when first He spoke to them of the Bread of Life, they have now disappeared in this moment of stupendous intimacy. New light dawns upon their minds, new love is born in their hearts, they are introduced in to a unity of vision with Jesus which makes them capable of surmounting reason and of seeing what it is that He has done. They can now behold how wisdom has achieved her ideal. Jesus is the Son of God. He has come down from heaven and taken unto Himself the flesh and blood of man. This is to be the sacrifice by which He will make the Godhead accessible to men. But before that sacrifice is made, and in view of it, Jesus, the Bread from Heaven, makes Himself the Food of men. He is a mighty Food, Food of angels and of men, and by His power He takes them to Himself to share with Him the very Life of Godhead. " I am the food of the grown," said Saint Augustine, " grow and thou shalt partake of this food ; nor shalt thou change me into thee, as thou dost thy corporeal food, but thou shalt be changed into me." This is an authentic echo of the words of Jesus : " The bread that I will give is my flesh, for the life of the world . . . He that eateth my flesh and drinketh my blood, abideth in me and I

in him. He that eateth me, the same shall live by me."
In truth the sharing with Him, by grace, in the life of Godhead
has begun.

Can we wonder that the memory of such a night, a memory
which He wished to be kept sacred, should linger in the heart
of humanity ? It was a night intended for men in every
clime and age, the night which lives and in which the Son of
God renews the gifts of Incarnation, Redemption, and of
Himself as the Food of mortals. No sooner had the apostles
accepted from His sacred Hands the chalice of salvation than
it passed from one to the other. Out from the Cenacle it was
borne by them into humble houses where they celebrated the
" breaking of the bread " ; from humble houses into catacomb
and prison to be the Strength of Christians ; from catacomb
and prison it was brought to church and cathedral, down to
this living moment in which Jesus, Who sacrificed Himself in
the Passion, renews the gift and the sacrifice for all generations.
What He did on that occasion for all He still does now for
each and for the self-same end, which is resurrection and life.
If the beloved Disciple was privileged to find peace upon
the breast of Jesus, it is Jesus Himself Who now seeks peace
upon the breast of a disciple.

IV.

In days to come the minds of these men would return
to the last moments of the Saviour's life on earth. Possessed
of His very Spirit they would be able to enter more fully into
the significance of His every gesture on that solemn night.
In particular their attention would be riveted on the chosen
means by which wisdom had, through Jesus, achieved her
ends. The Master had chosen the humble elements by which
the life of man on earth is nourished. He took account
of the fact that man is body as well as spirit. Life depends
on nourishment. There is only one form of life which contains
within itself its own sustenance—the Life of Godhead. The
Godhead is, in fact, the eternal Bethlehem wherein the Bread of
Life is born. When we raise our minds in a thought like this
a new significance is found in every gesture of our blessed

Lord. The words of the *Lauda Sion* come to mind : The Bread of Angels. Have you ever pictured to yourself the feeding of Angels ? Angels are pure spirits whose nourishment is truth. When they were admitted to a destiny beyond their natural powers the truth that was natural to them was not enough ; they had to be nourished by the Word of God, the self-same Word Who is now the Food of men. Like so many lakes of water, fed by rays from the living sun, angels became lightsome with the Word of God. Without that Word they should die of seeing the majesty of Light Inaccessible : neither angel nor man could see God and live. It is impossible then to ignore the condescension of Jesus Who adapts Himeelf to man's condition and approaches Him under the appearances of bread and wine.

For such a loving condescension there is but a single word in our vocabulary, the word compassion. Compassion means to suffer with and it was because Jesus in His love suffered with all men that He knew so well the only Food that could sustain them. It may be objected that compassion means pain, suffering as it does with others, and that Jesus glorious as He now is, is no longer capable of pain or suffering. But is it not a fact that Jesus actually did suffer in His mortal life ? His perfectly fashioned body, the refinement of His temperament that owed so much to the most perfect woman that ever existed, the marvellously close union in Him of soul and body—all these were factors in His extreme capacity for suffering. He knew men's emotions precisely because He Himself was fully human and because He experienced them in His life. Not only did He suffer, but He suffered as the Son of Man, that is, He suffered in Himself the sufferings of all men. The divine insight that was His made it possible for Him to anticipate our afflictions and our sorrows so that it was in fact the cry of our suffering that was on His lips, it was the tears of our anguish that were in His eyes, because it was the weight of our affliction that was weighing down His Sacred Heart. In compassion there are two elements : the love which is its life and the actual suffering which true compassion engenders in beings composed of soul and body. Of these two elements it is evident that love, the life and inspiration of compassion, is the more important. But at the source of the compassion of Jesus there is a love so unutterable that it fills His soul with tenderness, a tenderness born of His union with our nature. The Eucharist is a proof of love so personal that it makes us one with Jesus and thus brings home to us the fact that He experiences, as it were, the very heart-beat of our human feelings, the pulse of our hidden trials, the dejection of our human desolation. The soul, while it is in the body, experiences the feelings of the body. But no human soul is more united to human body than is Jesus to human souls when in Holy Communion He unites Himself to us : " He that eateth My flesh and drinketh My blood abideth in me and I in him." Is it not as if daily He renews the mystery of the Real Presence in human tabernacles, so that He should give enduring proof of His compassion.

Jesus had often referred to the Presence by which He would abide with His Church. At the Last Supper He did two marvellous things : He gave to the Church the power of the Real Presence ; He made the promise of the Spirit. These two things were not unrelated in the Master's mind. Both refer to a Presence : the one, to His Presence in the holy Eucharist ; the other, to His Presence in the Spirit. The exact relation between the two is what we must seek to grasp. The Spirit will minister to the Real Presence ; the Real Presence ministers to the Spirit's needs. The Spirit ministers to the Real Presence because it is the Spirit Who teaches the nascent Church the sigificance of the Eucharist and it is a fact of history that men and women have, through the Spirit's power, penetrated and tasted with experimental knowledge the reality of the Real Presence. On the other hand, the Eucharist ministers to the Spirit in human conditions because it keeps alive the flame of charity which the Holy Spirit brought to earth. The holy Eucharist is, in fact, the sacrament of unity by which the Church is held together in the unity of a mystic Body.

To the extent that men refuse this Food, there will be dissensions, hatreds, hostilities, and wars. And if the Heart of Jesus is saddened as it was on that occasion when He wept over the City of Jerusalem, His compassion has also the consolation of seeing His mystic Body. In a world shaken by forces of chaos and disruption, in an age of divided loyalties when men are torn asunder by forces of enmity and discord, when the Church is battling for the Cause of Religion, the eyes of Christ are gladdened by this sight. In human minds there is a common Faith which makes one the minds of many ; in human breasts there is one glorious hope, a hope that triumphs over death and dissolution ; surging through the entire body, and breaking down the barriers of individual isolatedness, there is a stream of life, of life whose one resplendent Source is Christ Himself. Upon the face of this new humanity God sees the glory of His Son, Jesus, and is glad.

VII

Resurrection.

I.

The life of man is a star in the night of creation lit by an almighty Hand. Its light leaps up in that mysterious moment when God infuses into human flesh a soul that is spiritual, incorruptible and immortal. Human life then is no chance-appearance, no meteoric flash, destined finally to disappear in utter darkness. It is a light lit as a witness to the purposiveness of God in all created things, a light destined for the eternal skies of undying life.

The result of almighty and creative Power, this life of man enjoys no enduring splendour amidst the changing scenes of earth. For a few short years it shines like a sun through the cloud of a human body. Its mysterious presence you may behold in the dewy freshness that blooms on childhood's limbs ; the rays of its beauty pierce through the bodies of men and women ; and then at last it goes down in death to leave in the world and in human hearts a darkness and a void.

That is but one image of human life : there are many others. Life is a fragile thing. It is a taper lit by God, a delicate flame set in the lamp of a human body. The body freely sacrifices its fund of oil to feed that flame. But the oil that sustains it in the body is not unlimited. Sooner or later the flame begins to flicker, and is finally extinguished. Sometimes a little gust of wind, an accident, is enough to put it out. Once extinguished, there is not a power on earth that is capable of re-lighting it. The body is cast away, like a thing outworn, into the darkness of the earth.

A few discordant voices have in recent times despairingly
proclaimed that the grave is the end of everything, when

> Human time
> Shall fold its eyelids, and the human sky
> Be gathered like a scroll within the tomb
> Unread for ever.

For them no eternal life exists. They have peered into the
future and seen the eclipse of life, of all the labour of the
ages, of all the devotion and inspiration and noonday brightness
of human genius, in a vast death of our solar system.
Scientific research, which has so greatly extended our
knowledge of the material world, is mute when asked for
prophecies that relate to a future life. A thousand questions
the scientist can answer about the earth on which we live,
but ask him the vital question that has harassed the mind of
man in every age, that question which so intimately concerns
every one of us, the manner of our existence after death, and
the scientist of the twentieth century can only shake his head
in hopeless avowal of his ignorance.

Human wisdom as a whole, whether it be sought from
science or literature or philosophy, can boast no final or
satisfying solution of this enigma. Thinkers there have been
who clearly saw that death could not be the end, that there is in
human structure a spiritual element which, naturally
indestructible, must outlive the body, an immortal soul.
They have deepened this conviction by consulting the depths
of man's spiritual desire and concluded that unless the
universe entire is meaningless, the vast material world must
have a spiritual counterpart. Man would be a sorry mockery
if his deep desire of enduring life were to be frustrated in the
end ; he would be the dupe of virtue if no future life existed
in which to compensate the just and punish the wicked ;
his instinctive dread of the sleep of death

> For in that sleep of death what dreams may come
> When we have shuffled off this mortal coil
> Must give us pause

is witness to a spirit that is made for eternal horizons. But
as to the manner of the satisfaction of man's deep desires, the

kind of existence this future life will be, human philosophy can afford no confident answer. There is one thing that human wisdom could have never known, the destiny of the human body. As far as human thinking is concerned, the darkness of earth must be its abiding home.

Such is not our Christian hope. As we stand in awe and trembling on this earth of graves, where to live is constantly to be faced with death which can trample human bodies to dust and ashes, there is a voice across the centuries which bids us hope, the voice heard by the Apostle John, upon the island of Patmos. "And I saw a new heaven and a new earth. For the first heaven and the first earth was gone, and the sea is now no more . . . and God shall wipe away all tears from their eyes : and death shall be no more. Nor mourning, nor crying, nor sorrow shall be any more for the former things are passed away. And he that sat upon the throne said : Behold I make all things new. And he said to me : Write, for these words are most faithful and true." [1]

In the light of this prophetic vision we can behold God at work, lighting the torch of life again in human bodies, and preparing for man's eternal dwelling-place " a new heaven and a new earth." He at Whose creative Word the universe sprang into being, He Who first lighted the stars in the firmament, He Who is the unfailing Source of life has promised not only a survival of the spirit and immortality, but a resurrection. Then death shall be no more, and human bodies will no longer lie in the cold darkness of the earth. Not only shall human spirits live, but there will be that wedding of body and spirit, that reconstitution of man in the integrity of his nature, so that human bodies shall share in the beatific joy of souls in that recreation of the world mysteriously suggested by the words " a new heaven and a new earth."

This is the authentic Christian hope, the hope of a complete and radical triumph of life over death, a victory which involves an entire cosmic change and the resurrection of human bodies for life in a world to come. That is the hope

[1] Apoc. xxi, 1, 4, 5.

which takes from death its lasting sting, for pain shall be no more, and tears shall be wiped away, and bodies shall participate in the ecstacy of spirit. It were vain to suggest the exultation of such a life. There are moments of our earthly existence when, touched by superlative beauty, we are lifted out of the stream of time, when for a moment body is converted into soul, the universe has become a species of music entirely harmonious, moments when we seem to have entered some heaven of intoxicating delight, and these are but shadows of the reality which they prefigure. " Eye hath not seen, nor ear heard ; neither hath it entered into the heart of man, what things God hath prepared for them that love Him." [1] It is more to our present purpose to examine carefully the foundation of our hope.

II.

So intimate a part of our inheritance, so accepted a formula of belief, has this glorious hope become that the splendour of it may be a little dimmed. If we would appreciate the magnificence of it, the precision with which it is expressed by our Saviour Jesus, we must compare it not only with the teachings of the unenlightened mind of the natural man, but with the great prophetic utterances of the men of God under the ancient Dispensation. We shall then be prepared to look with new eyes upon Him Who declared Himself the Resurrection, and realise more vividly that the foundation of our hope is Jesus Christ Who in death merited for humanity eternal life, and Who in rising from the dead became not only the prototype and exemplar of all resurrection but the Cause by Whose efficacy we shall, like Him, rise gloriously from the tomb of death.

It was an essential part of His message that the vision of God in a future life was the actual destiny of mankind. Of that vision there were certain intimations in the original revelation made by God. From the time of Jacob the idea had become in a sense traditional, but to this day interpreters will dispute the exact character of this vision. The attitude

[1] 1 Cor., ii, 9.

of the Old Testament writers is not unequivocal. The vision imparted to Jacob, Moses, Isaiah, Ezechiel is hedged around with reservations and is accompanied by such a wealth of imagery that the precise meaning of their experience is not easily decided.[1] There are explicit statements to the effect that no man can see God and live, and the tribe of Levi, we are told, disappeared for having seen Him. It is by no means certain that the vision of God spoken of was really vision, and more often it is to be taken to mean that more vivid consciousness of Him in the chosen place of worship. When the psalmist sings of his desire of seeing God, he is thinking not infrequently of the privilege of being in the Temple to enjoy God's special presence.

When it is a question no longer of the present life but of the future life in which this vision might be expected really to be consummated, it is not difficult to see a certain hesitation in the Old Testament. There was a very good reason for such an attitude. The memory of the chosen people was filled with the expulsion of Adam and Eve from the paradise of delight. Created by God immortal, endowed with original justice, man ruined his hopes of life by sin, and the sense of sin, with the consequence of death, was there to colour the outlook of the holy prophets. There are moments when the prospect of life after death is dark enough, as when the holy man, Job, cried out : " Shall not the fewness of my days be ended shortly ? Suffer me, therefore, that I may lament my sorrow a little : Before I go, and return no more, to a land that is dark and covered with the mist of death . . . . and no order but everlasting horror dwelleth." [2] We cannot miss the sense of annihilation which echoes from certain phrases of the Psalmist : " For there is no one in death that is mindful of Thee : and who shall confess Thee in hell ? " [3] " What profit is there in my blood, whilst I go down to corruption ? Shall dust confess to Thee, or declare Thy Truth ? " [4]

[1] Cf. Gen., xxxii, 30 ; Exod., xxxiii, 11 ; Ezech., x, 18 ; Num., xii, 6–8.
[2] Job, x, 20–22.
[3] Ps., vi, 6.
[4] Ps., xxix, 10.

These forbodings are made an excuse for emphasis on the
present life in an appeal for longevity, on the plea that
little good accrues to God from those who die.   The dead
are " Like the slain sleeping in the sepulchres whom Thou
rememberest no more : and they are cast off from Thy hand " [1]
whereas the living can at least praise the Almighty : " The
dead shall not praise Thee, O Lord : nor any of them that go
down to hell.   But we that live bless the Lord : from this time
now and forever " [2] What is certain from the Old Testament
is that though a future life exists, there is an exclusion from
eternal life, and the nature and conditions of this future life
are dim and obscure. [3]

This does not mean that gleams of anticipation are entirely
absent.   It is impossible to follow the general movement of
the psalms without the conviction that the ultimate ideal is
the seeing of God face to face, and in that ideal the implicit
affirmation of human immortality.   The Psalmist returns
frequently to the theme of spiritual aspiration, he may have
in mind the Temple in which he can worship the God of truth,
but it is equally clear that he has the conviction that the
Lord will not consign to corruption the soul of His faithful
worshipper : " For thou wilt not abandon me to the under-
world ; Nor wilt thou permit thy faithful worshipper to see
destruction.   Thou wilt show me the way of life ; Thou
wilt fill me with joy through the vision of Thee.   Delights
are in Thy right hand for ever." [4] More clearly still, there
is the hope expressed : " But I shall appear in justice before
Thee : I shall be sated when Thy glory reveals itself." [5]
In this it is clearly stated in the original Hebrew that the
prophet will see the Face of God, and that he well be sated
when he awakes (from death) by the vision of God. [6]

A similar vision is to be found in the prophet Isaiah,
wherein the anticipation of the Seer of Patmos is more

---

[1] Ps., lxxxvii, 6.

[2] Ps., cxiii, 17–18.

[3] See Gen., xxv, 6–10 ; Job, xiv, 13–17.

[4] Ps., xv, 10–11.   This is the translation made by Dr. Boylan, *The Psalms*.
A Study of the Vulgate Psalter in the Light of the Hebrew Text, vol. I, p. 50–52.

[5] Ps. xvi, 15.

[6] Boylan, M.A., D.D., D.Litt., op. cit., p. 57.

pointedly made. Isaiah declared centuries before : " He shall cast death down headlong for ever : and the Lord God shall wipe away tears from every face, and the reproach of his people. He shall take away from off the whole earth : for the Lord hath spoken it." [1] But the greatest light in the darkness of pre-Christian days shines forth from a few words uttered by the holy man of God, Job, in the darkness of his tribulations : " For I know that My Redeemer liveth, and in the last day I shall rise out of the earth. And I shall be clothed again with my skin, and in my flesh I shall see my God. Whom I myself shall see and my eyes shall behold, and not another ; this my hope is laid up in my bosom." [2] The Church has made her own the glorious affirmation of Job, and we can never read such words without thinking of the dictum of St. Jerome that " no man since the days of Christ has so clearly spoken of resurrection as this man, Job, who lived years before the coming of Christ." [3]

The word " redeemer " is significant. In Hebrew usage it designated one who should avenge the wrongs of the oppressed and vindicate their rights. Considering the people's awareness of sin, of the fact that they were under the judgment of God, it is easy to see that " redeemer " might have a deeper meaning. Jesus, as His name suggests, was Saviour. The Angel had explicitly said to Joseph : "And she shall bring forth a son ; and thou shalt call His name Jesus. For he shall save his people from their sins." [4] In the very moment of the Incarnation He presented Himself to the Father in the joyous will to save the world by His passion and death : " Sacrifice and oblation thou wouldst not : but a body thou hast fitted to me : holocausts for sin did not please thee. Then said I : Behold I come : in the head of the book it is written of me : that I should do thy will, O God." [5] That first oblation was the inspiration of the Master's every action, the theme to all His life on earth, and it is with reason that

[1] Isa., xxv, 8.

[2] Job, xix, 25–27.

[3] Cf. Fillion, Cl., L., *Ll sainte bible, Commentee*, t. iii, pp. 548–550.

[4] Matt., i, 21.

[5] Heb., x, 5.

Saint Bonaventure cries out in admiration : " I will not name that day on which He dies as the passion of my Saviour, for His whole life, from beginning to end, was an example and a martyrdom."

It is in the light of this vision of redemption ever before His eyes, though as yet hidden from others, that we must approach the revelation which Jesus made to Martha at the grave of Lazarus. This revelation took place at Bethany, that place of refuge not far from Jerusalem, where Jesus found human hearts that understood and appreciated Him. Saint John describes Bethany as "the town of Mary and Martha her sister" and the incident took place before the Master's final visit to Jerusalem. It was at a time when His life was menaced by the Jews and He had left Judea for a period. But the Sisters of Bethany were able to get in touch with Him and when Lazarus fell ill they sent the message : " Lord, behold, he whom thou lovest is sick." [1] The message made no suggestion of a return because the people who sent it knew the circumstances of His departure and it was enough, they knew, to appeal to His Heart. "It is enough for You to know," as Saint Augustine interprets their thoughts, " for You do not love and then abandon." Did Jesus send back an answer or did He merely say to those around Him : " This sickness is not unto death, but for the glory of God : that the Son of God may be glorified by it?" [2] What is certain is that the disciples did not grasp the significance of the promise.

Assuming that He was a little less than two days' journey from Bethany, Lazarus was already dead when the message reached Him. But the disciples were reassured on hearing that the sleep of Lazarus was not unto death. Imagine their surprise when, two days later, the Master suddenly said to them : " Let us go into Judea again." [3] To return so soon, they felt, was to risk certain death and in their anxiety for His safety they said to Him : " Rabbi, the Jews but now sought to stone thee : and goest thou thither again ? " [4]

[1] John, xi, 3.
[2] *Ibid*, xi, 4.
[3] John, xi, 7.
[4] *Ibid*, xi, 8.

What they did not know was that in the meantime Lazarus
had died and Jesus now told them in words that have become
immortal : " Lazarus our friend sleepeth." [1]   Even then the
disciples did not understand.   He had to tell them brusquely :
" Lazarus is dead.   And I am glad, for your sakes, that I was
not there, that you may believe : but, let us go to him." [2]
The suggestion is that had He been there He could not have
resisted the Sisters' appeal.   But He was glad for the sake
of His disciples that it had not been so.   That was the
moment when Thomas uttered those words from which we
cannot withold our admiration : " Let us also go, that we may
die with Him." [3]

Meanwhile what was happening at Bethany ?   What were
the thoughts and feelings of the two Sisters ?   Had word
come to them that the illness was not unto death we can
imagine their perplexity when Lazarus died.   Though they
thought it was now too late for effective aid, they still
expected Him and knew instinctively that, in spite of danger,
He would come.   When news of His approach reached them,
Martha went out to meet Him : " Lord, if thou hadst been
here, my brother had not died."   The words, so outspoken,
were half reproach and half excuse, though she quickly added :
" But now also I know that whatsoever thou wilt ask of God,
God will give it thee." [4]   She was not thinking of the raising
of Lazarus from the dead.   Such a possibility does not seem
to have entered her head.   Even when Jesus said, " Thy
brother shall rise again," she merely replied : " I know that
he shall rise again, in the resurrection at the last day."   This
in itself was significant as pointing to the Master's accepted
teaching but there was something more.   According to
Jewish belief, some of the just were in Paradise and some
were in what was called " Shoel " which would correspond
to the Christian Purgatory.   If Lazarus was young and
unmarried, the current view was that such a premature death
was due to sin so that he was in " Shoel."   This perhaps was

[1] *Ibid*, xi, 11.
[2] *Ibid*, xi, 14, 15.
[3] *Ibid*, xi, 16.
[4] John, xi, 22.

what was in the mind of Martha when she declared her belief in the Master's power with God. However that may be, her response evoked from Jesus the most triumphant affirmation ever uttered by human lips : " I am the resurrection and the life : he that believeth in me, although he be dead, shall live : and every one that liveth, and believeth in me, shall not die for ever." [1] Martha accepted His words and said : " Yea, Lord, I have believed that thou art Christ the Son of the living God, who art come into this world." Did Martha fully enter into the thought she had just expressed ? Did she realise that faith in Jesus is a beginning made in eternal life ? It sufficed that she accepted Jesus Who is the Resurrection and the Life.

This incident alone would suffice to indicate the Master's attitude to a future life. There was one other occasion when those who believed that death was the end of everything gave Him an opportunity of making clear His teaching on immortality. He referred to the life beyond the present world when human persons shall continue to exist but in a higher manner—like the angels—and left no room for doubt as to the reality of a future existence when the good shall be rewarded and the wicked punished. But if we wish to find the simplest, and most beautiful, presentation of His doctrine we must assist at that last meeting of the Master with His disciples in the Supper-room. It was then that, like the Son He was, He dispelled the mists and shadows of the ages, that He gave shape and form to the unknown territory of immortality, and made their minds and hearts converge upon Him, the Resurrection and the Life.

In that hour of tremendous intimacy, putting from Him the cares of the morrow, He broached the vital question which has harassed the human mind in every age. " Let not your heart be troubled. You believe in God; believe also in me." [2] That was the key-note to all that followed, a note sustained by love and power and light. " In my Father's house there are many mansions. If not, I would have told you : because I go

[1] John, xi, 25, 26.
[2] John, xiv, 1.

to prepare a place for you." [1]   He was suggesting to them a departure and He was suggesting His Lordship over the unknown.   The departure was to be a brief one, a stepping from one mansion to another in the universe of God, and He would not leave them waiting long : "A little while, and now you shall not see me ; and again a little while, and you shall see me ; because I go to the Father." [2]   At that moment He had warmed their hearts with His Presence and awakened their desire ever to be with Him.   They fully trusted Him now : He knew it.   He could tell them of the step that all must take, the crossing of the threshold.   " Men fear death as children fear to go into the dark."   But Jesus would go first, He is the Way, and He would return to them.   He is telling them before the event what death is.   In the days to come they would realise it.   They would have seen that the manner of his going was death ; and that the manner of His coming was resurrection.   Could anything be more simple or more touching ?   There was nothing left for Him to do except to verify His prophecy, and securely establish in their hearts the hope that when the supreme moment came, near or distant, He would return for them : "And if I shall go, and prepare a place for you, I will come again, and will take you to myself : that where I am, you also may be." [3]

III.

To enter fully into this teaching of the Master it is necessary to bring together the two ideas suggested by death and resurrection in the unity of redemption ; they are really complementary.   On the Cross He was immolated, as the true Lamb of God, for the sins of the world.   Sin was the original cause of spiritual death from which flowed the death of the body.   The death of Jesus, so lovingly accepted by Him in expiation, was intended to destroy the very death which lay at the root of all human misery.   That was not enough. He wished to ensure the application of this objective

[1] *Ibid*, 2.
[2] *Ibid*, xvi, 16.
[3] John, xiv, 3.

redemption which He wrought upon the Cross. The means of doing so was the resurrection. Therefore must He rise from the dead, and be in fact the first-born of the dead, so that He, the Prince of Life, might become the Source of Life for all humanity. For as no man cometh to the Father except by the mediation of the Son, so new life cannot descend from God to man except through the mediation of the Man-God. The death on Calvary was but one aspect of redemption; the resurrection was the necessary complement.

St. Thomas makes the point with his usual lucidity. Allowing for the fact that the death of our blessed Saviour was the meritorious cause of man's salvation, he says that the resurrection must be looked upon as the efficient cause of man's birth to new life, and, ultimately, resurrection. It is necessary to stress this efficacy of the resurrection, an efficacy that results from the fact that the humanity of Jesus becomes, in the resurrection, "a quickening spirit." [1] St. Paul explicitly says that Jesus was delivered up for our sins ·and that He rose again for our justification. [2] It is this which St. Thomas has in mind when he goes on to explain the point at issue. "Properly speaking, Christ's resurrection is not the meritorious cause, but the efficient and exemplary cause of our resurrection. It is the efficient cause, in as much as Christ's humanity, according to which He rose again, is as it were the instrument of His Godhead, and works by its power. And therefore, just as all other things which Christ did and endured in His humanity are profitable to our salvation through the power of the Godhead, so also is Christ's resurrection the efficient cause of ours, through the divine power whose office it is to quicken the dead; and this power by its presence is in touch with all places and times; and such virtual contact suffices for its efficiency." [3]

Seeing the great honour that accrues to the sacred Humanity, one begins to see new significance in the very depths of His passion and death and the divine assurance that

[1] 1 Cor., xv, 45.
[2] Rom., iv, 25.
[3] *Summa*, IIIa Pars., Q. lvi, a–i, ad3.

His Humanity, which suffered so much, would rise triumphant and enter upon a still higher phase of existence, a mode of being and action so completely transfused by the power of His Divinity that it would share, as it were, in the prerogatives of Godhead and extend its life-giving influence throughout space and time. Was He not anxious, after resurrection, that they should not only verify the truth of the fact, but that they should also glimpse something of this glorifying of His Humanity. Though Jesus becomes a " quickening spirit," he does not merely become a spirit, for He rises with a spiritualised Body.

One has only to read St. Luke's account to appreciate this. The report is so perfect that it must be given just as it is, " Now whilst they were speaking these things, Jesus stood in the midst of them, and saith to them : Peace be to you : it is I, fear not. But they being troubled and frightened, supposed that they saw a spirit. And he said to them : "Why are you troubled, and why do thoughts arise in your hearts ? See my hands and feet, that it is I myself ; handle, and see : for a spirit hath not flesh and bones, as you see me to have." And when he had said this, he shewed them his hands and feet. But while they yet believed not, and wondered for joy, he said : " Have you here anything to eat ? " And they offered him a piece of a broiled fish, and a honeycomb. And when he had eaten before them, taking the remains, he gave to them. And he said to them : " These are the words which I spoke to you, while I was yet with you, that all things must needs be fulfilled, which are written . . . Thus it is written, and thus it behoved Christ to suffer, and to rise again from the dead, the third day." [1] What before His death He had promised, and foretold, He offered now to their experimental knowledge, the feeling and the touching of His very Body, so evident particularly in the case of the doubting Thomas. [2]

This life-giving role of the sacred Humanity in resurrection gives point to the contrast which is so frequent

[1] Luke, xxiv, 36–46.
[2] John, xx, 27.

in the writings of St. Paul, the contrast between the first
Adam, who was the source of death, and the second Adam,
Jesus, Who is the source of life and resurrection. The
Apostle expresses the contrast vividly : " The first man, Adam
was made into a living soul ; the last Adam into a quickening
spirit." [1] If we consider this contrast for a moment, we
shall have a clearer vision of the vivifying influence of the
risen Christ.

In the inspired account of origins by Genesis, which can
never be surpassed, man was fashioned out of the slime of
the earth, and God breathed into his face the breath of life
so that man became a " living soul." [2] However science
may fill out this history of man, the teaching must remain
that the human soul, the formal perfection by which man is
what he is, is directly from God. This soul fulfils two
functions : first, it gives life to the human body as its
animating principle ; second, it utilises the body in the interest
of a higher life which belongs to it as mind or spirit. In
this way it is seen that man differs from the animal because
his soul is spiritual, and he differs from pure spirits because
spirits do not animate bodies ; they are not souls. The
soul of man is the only kind of soul that is spiritual ; and it
is the only kind of spirit that is a soul ; that is, the animating
principle of a body. Over and above the natural life,
implied in this stricture of body and spirit, man received,
by the sheer munificence of God, a supernatural life of grace
which was nothing less than a sharing, as from within, in
God's own life. When God created him [3] He said : " Let
us make man to our image and likeness," [3] and the Hebrew
text refers to a superlative form of resemblance which can
be understood only in terms of grace, as is clearly suggested
by St. John : "We know that when he shall appear we shall
be like to him : because we shall see him as he is." [4]

The continued participation in the Life of God by grace
was made contingent upon man's obedience, and Adam

[1] 1 Cor., xv, 45.
[2] Gen., ii, 7.
[3] Gen., i, 26.
[4] 1 John, iii, 2.

possessed this life as the appointed head of the human race. "But of the tree of knowledge of good and evil," said God, "thou shalt not eat. For in what day soever thou shalt eat of it, thou shalt die the death." [1] The effect of disobedience was precisely the loss of the higher life ; Adam and Eve were driven forth from the garden of innocence ; an Angel with a flaming sword, turning every way, "kept the tree of life ; " and they found themselves in nakedness before God, deprived of the life of grace which had adorned their souls. In the course of time corporeal death made its first appearance on the earth.

In this account the natural dependence of man, a living soul, upon the earth is indicated. Not only was he of the earth, with senses that put him in living contact with the earth, but the animal nature which was his, drew sustenance for life from things around him. This dependence upon the things of sense was intensified by the Fall. If we represent to ourselves the spiritual being of man as a pyramid, with its point facing towards the earth, we can see that it is a kind of wedge which is more deeply driven into the world of matter as dependence upon the world of sense increases. To lift him out of the plight into which he plunged himself by sin man needed the redemption and resurrection of the Saviour.

Jesus is the new Adam. As all were born to an earthly existence of the first Adam, so men are born to the higher life through the vivifying influence of Jesus Christ. If the first Adam was created by God "a living soul," Jesus in rising from the dead became "a quickening spirit." It is true that at all times Jesus was the Source of life, the Resurrection and the Life, but He was content, in the interests of redemption, to accept mortality so that, dying willingly for sin, He should become in His resurrection the vivifying and quickening influence upon which is founded all hope of future resurrection. The transfiguration of His human nature, which He allowed three privileged Apostles to behold in life, became the permanent state after resurrection wherein the sacred Humanity drew all its life from the Godhead in Him.

[1] Gen., ii, 17.

Since Christ is thus the Head of the new humanity, His resurrection is the prototype and exemplar of all resurrection. In Him already, in a sense, humanity, and all things of which humanity is an epitome, has risen from the dead. But this potential resurrection in Him must become actual in His members. So intimate is the connection between the risen Christ and humanity which, by right, belongs to Him that St. Paul argues from the resurrection of Christ to that of Christians and from the denial of Christian resurrection to the denial of that of Jesus Christ. Of all men Christians are most miserable who would believe only in the present life, for while others make the most of passing things, the Christian is one who is ready to lay down his life in defence of his Christian Faith. But if the present life is the supreme good for man, then there is no reason for sacrificing it. " For if the dead rise not again, neither is Christ risen again. And if Christ be not risen again, your faith is vain ; for you are yet in your sins. Then they also that are fallen asleep in Christ, are perished. If in this life only we have hope in Christ, we are of all men most miserable. But now Christ is risen from the dead, the first fruits of them that sleep : For by a man came death, and by a man the resurrection of the dead. And as in Adam all die, so also in Christ all shall be made alive." [1]

IV.

The mystery of Resurrection is, in truth, a diamond of many facets. It flashes the glory of its light upon human existence in all directions. Now it suffuses the present life with light and hope ; now its rays penetrate the veils of time and space which hide from us the world of immortality. The more deeply we look into it, the more is there to be seen, and eyes that are strengthened by living faith can find the heart of its glory : it is a message about death, death that has been vanquished and destroyed.

Can you wonder that St. Paul, for whom the resurrection was so vivid, could sing the greatest lyric to Death ever sung

[1] 1 Cor., xv, 16–22.

by human lips ?　As we think of this glory the rays of which
light up the dark unknown territory of the future, his words
spring spontaneously to our lips : " There is the glory of the
sun, and the glory of the moon, and the glory of the stars ;
for star differeth from star in glory.　What is sown in
corruption doth rise in incorruption ; what is sown in
dishonour doth rise in glory ; what is sown in weakness doth
rise in power ; what is sown in a natural body doth rise a
spiritual body.　For the trumpet shall sound, and the dead
shall rise incorruptible, and we shall be changed.　For this
corruptible body must needs put on incorruption, and this
mortal body immortality.　And when this mortal body
shall put on immortality, shall come to pass the word which
is written : Death is swallowed up in victory.　Death, where
is thy victory ?　Death, where is thy sting ? " [1]

When Jesus died, death was dead ; when Jesus rose
again, eternal life was made accessible to men.　The
disciples had seen him die.　They scarcely knew what to make
of His promises and His prophecies.　But in the sealed tomb
of death the miracle took place.　Coming on Easter morning,
they found the tomb empty, the cloths carefully laid on one
side, and they believed.[2]　That same evening, as they were
gathered together He stood in their midst and showed them
His hands and His feet.　Jesus had returned to them as He
said He would, and it was no longer a question of words and
prophecies but of fact and of fulfilment.　Jesus, now no longer
of this earth, remained upon it, to give them a vision of the
world to come.　He appeared to them as One in Whom
beatitude was already a fact ; they had heaven before their
eyes.　All they had to do was to look at Him, to listen to Him,
to touch and feel Him : He was in truth the great Immortal,
the Resurrection, in Whom they could see what exactly lay
in store for them when death had done its mightiest in them.

That was not the only purpose of this revelation.　Jesus
was thinking of the present life.　He showed Himself
" alive after His passion, by many proofs, for forty days

[1] Cf. 1 Cor., xv, 41.
[2] John, xx, 8.

appearing to them, and speaking of the kingdom of God. And eating together with them, he commanded them, that they should not depart from Jerusalem, but should wait for the promise of the Father, which you have heard (saith he) by my mouth. For John indeed baptised with water, but you shall be baptised with the Holy Ghost, not many days hence."[1] If His resurrection was to be effective for the life of humanity, it was imperative that these men should first receive the Spirit of life, that they should awaken, in Pentecost, to the Kingdom of God within them and think no longer of a mere restoration of Israel but of the whole world to be transformed into a kingdom of life and love and truth.

If any man thinks he can account for these Apostles, Peter and John and the rest, except by the miracle of the risen Christ, he is deceiving himself. They became what they did become because their hearts were kindled by that vision, and because in time they received the Spirit in Whose power they went forth to evangelise the world. It was in the name of Jesus, in the very Person of Jesus, that they went forth. The theme of their preaching was the risen Christ, and their triumphant argument was that they simply could not but speak the things they had seen and heard.[2] In them Jesus, Whom enemies had thought to destroy, inaugurated an existence on earth that will endure until the end of time.

The first great conversion to Christianity was a witness to this. The Pharisee, Saul, endeavouring to exterminate the community of the Christians was met on his way by the risen Christ Who said to him : " I am Jesus whom thou persecutest." So did Saul learn of the identity of Christ and the Church which is His sacrament on earth. When Saul was converted into Paul, his aim also was to marshal his witnesses, from Peter to himself, in evidence of the risen Christ. The Corinthians of his day he challenged with the great alternative of the risen Christ or a Christian Faith that is without foundation. To those who considered themselves wise, imagining that the resurrection of the body was a thing

[1] Acts, i, 3–5.
[2] See John, iii, 11, 32.

impossible, he gave the crushing reply : " Senseless man, that which thou sowest is not quickened except it die first. And that which thou sowest, thou sowest not the body that shall be ; but bare grain, as of wheat, or of some of the rest." [1]

The argument was a sound one. Besides being reminiscent of a celebrated dictum of Christ Himself, it pointed to a general law of things where death is seen to be a condition of life. But there was the further point, that men who could not understand how the harvest comes from the death of seeds in the earth had little right to object to the Christian view of the resurrection of the body. The power of God is not forshortened. The same Spirit Who gave life to the dead Body of Jesus is certainly capable of giving life to the bodies of His followers : " But God giveth it a body as he will : and to every seed its proper body." [2]

St. Paul was well aware of man's deep aspiration for immortality. With belief in the resurrection of the body he was able to give that aspiration its full expression. " Yea, in this present abode we groan, yearning to be clothed over with the dwelling-place that is from heaven, if, indeed, we shall be found clothed at all and not naked. For we who are in this tabernacle then groan under our burden because we would fain not be unclothed : but rather clothed over, that what is mortal may be swallowed up by life." [3] He would not have the Christians act as if this glorious hope was not a precious possession. The Thessalonians, he found, were indulging immoderate grief over their dead. It was not that they were ignorant of the doctrine of Resurrection, but that they had not made of it a living hope which ought to suffuse the lives of Christians with light. He chided them with their failure, and forbade them to be like " those others who have no hope." [4] He was not forbidding them a reasonable sorrow, for that is natural and religion does not empty out the natural,

[1] 1 Cor., xv, 36, 37.
[2] *Ibid*, 38.
[3] Cf. 2 Cor., v, 2–4.
[4] 1 Thess, iv, 12.

but he was definitely excluding that dark and pagan outlook
which is the very negation of Resurrection.   To believe that
our glorious Saviour has risen from the dead is to believe
that the dead who die in Him shall also rise, that they are in
fact in possession of eternal life, so that the pagan outlook
for which the things of the spirit are shadowy and unreal is
resolutely excluded from the Christian mind.

" Know you not that all we, who are baptised in Christ
Jesus, are baptised in His death ?   For we are buried together
with him by baptism into death : that, as Christ is risen from
the dead by the glory of the Father, so we also may walk in
newness of life." [1]   The basis of our hope is incorporation
with Jesus, an incorporation which is begun in Baptism.   The
symbolism of the rite, the plunging in the water, signifies
the death of Jesus.   The death of Jesus was, we know, the
death of death, and to be incorporated with Him is to be in
living contact with eternal life.   Jesus is the Life not only
of those who walk the earth but of those who live in heaven
or in purgatory.   The more intimate our union with Him
Who is Life, the closer are we to our beloved dead who draw
their immortality, of bliss or of suffering, from Him.   The
only difference is one of vision ; they behold what we do
not as yet see, and their desire for us may be the cause of our
increasing vision, just as our desires for them may be the one
thing necessary to give them the vision which they so much
desire.   In truth our intimacy with the dead is unutterably
great, for it is the Jesus Who lives in us Who is either pouring
beatific joy into their souls in heaven or purifying their souls
for vision in purgatory.   In him the dead and we live and move
and have our being, and if He be near, can they be far off ?

This incorporation with Jesus has its aspirations and ideals.
St. Paul sums them up in a striking phrase : " If you be
risen with Christ, seek the things that are above . . . Mind the
things that are above, not the things that are upon the
earth." [2]   Do you know what that means ?   It means that
as we make progress in holiness we shall increasingly draw

[1] Rom., vi, 3, 4.
[2] Col., iii, 1.

nourishment from Him Who is our life, that the daily food of our lives shall be not only the bread of the body but the Bread of Life, and that ultimately we shall find in our souls a fire of desire for the things that are not of the earth. So shall we liberate the pyramid of our spiritual being from the earth which surrounds it, and discover that death, which is so hateful for the natural man, may assume an entirely new aspect. The new vision will be but the logical development of that happy night in us which is the Faith. It is then that, forgetting its earthly home, the soul will listen in its night for the word of the Bridegroom, "I will espouse thee to me for ever," and it will know that its night is now no more for "they shall not need the light of the lamp, nor the light of the sun, because the Lord God shall enlighten them, and they shall reign for ever and ever."[1]

[1] Apoc., xxii, 5.

VIII.

Pentecost.

I.

One of the most fascinating periods in the Master's ministry is that which lies between the Resurrection and the coming of the Spirit at Pentecost. So typical of our human estate is this mysterious period in the life of the Apostles, and so characteristic of loving initiative on the part of our blessed Lord that, by a kind of instinct, the mind returns to it in search of light. Jesus had summarised His life for them in words they thought they understood : " I came forth from the Father, and am come into the world : again I leave the world, and I go to the Father." [1] They were now to learn that, though the visible presence of the Master was taken from them in death, He was willing to stay on earth "a little while" [2] in order to complete the formation of His followers.

That formation had begun for the Apostles with the sudden disclosure of a mysterious and haunting holiness in the Face of Jesus. Saint Jerome does not fail to note that the ready response of the tax-gatherer, Matthew, was in answer to the splendour of Godhead hidden in Jesus. Similar evidence of a secret and divine a tractiveness might be sought for all the others. For a period of three years they were privileged to live in intimacy with the Perfect. During the course of that time many a change was wrought in their outlook and character. Strangely enough, at the end of it they were not fully formed. The Shepherd was struck and they were quickly scattered. The Resurrection found them either ignorant or incredulous.

[1] John, xvi, 28.
[2] John, xvi, 18.

110

It is not for us to censure these men so human. One thing stands to their immortal credit : they had obeyed the Call. From the serried ranks of a self-centred and deluded people they had stepped forth, ready to accept the Christ for what He might prove to be in fact and not merely for what they wanted Him to be. They offer a vivid contrast to the many others, who, recognising the superiority of Jesus, would not accept Him or submit their minds to His purposes. The proud and learned of the day would make use of Him for their own petty interests. Failing that, they insanely sought to rid the world of Him. Towards the end it was as if the frightful strain of His sinless presence proved too much for them. There are untold depths of wickedness in the avowal that lay hidden in the question : "What do we, for this man doth many miracles ? If we let him alone so, all will believe in him," [1] In that confession the Pharisees announced their own judgment. Saint John does not mince his words : "And this is the judgment : because the light is come into the world, and men loved the darkness rather than the light, for their works were evil." [2]

The Apostles did not hate the light. The Master found in them a sincere desire for Godliness. They shared the prejudices of their people, it is true, and the task of changing their outlook, of inspiring them with a new sense of values, was colossal. To this task Jesus brought a tenderness that was touching, a patience that was inexhaustible, a humility that must have been entirely disarming. Making Himself One of them, living their life, talking their language, He endeavoured to communicate to them His message in the simplest terms. It is not difficult to surmise the claims made upon His sensitiveness by this commerce, necessarily so one-sided, between Him and them. But Jesus was not One to think of human reactions where the interests of the Father were at stake. "And he that sent me," said Jesus, " is with me, and he hath not left me alone : for I do always the things that please him." [3] He found the Apostles receptive,

[1] John, xi, 47.
[2] John, iii, 19.
[3] John, viii, 29.

willing, ready to be moulded, transformed if necessary, by the virtue that went out from Him, the perfect Teacher.

One often wonders what were the real thoughts of these simple men. Jesus was One of them, but with a difference. There are moments when He towers in majesty above them and to this majesty of Him even enemies bear witness : " Never did man speak like this man." [1] Nicodemus had also argued : " For no man can do these signs which thou dost, unless God be with him." [2] But from avowals like these, even when they are not wrung from men, to a true, a constant, a living recognition of the sublime Reality of Jesus the distance was great. It is this distance, a distance that must be traversed if they are to enter into the mystery of their Master, which gives so poignant a character to the mission of our blessed Lord amongst His chosen ones. There are certain over-tones which, if one is sensitive, can be heard in His utterances, particularly towards the end. We are not now thinking of an occasion when, quite candidly, He told them : " You know not of what spirit you are." [3] Rather have we in mind the disappointment that shows itself so discreetly when He remarks that hitherto they had never asked the Father for anything in His name. They had lived with Him, had heard His affirmation of identity with the Father, and yet Philip says to Him : " Show us the Father." [4] Less in rebuke than in sorrow Jesus says : " Have I been so long a time with you ; and have you not known me ? " [5] And He goes on to explain : " If you had known me, you would without doubt have known my Father also. [6]

It is clear beyond a shadow of doubt that something vital was lacking to their knowledge of Him ; and this was on the very eve of His death. But think of the goodness of Jesus which prompts Him to submit so fully to the reality of His disciples. He is content to live with them for three years,

[1] John, vii, 46.
[2] John, iii, 2.
[3] Luke, ix, 55.
[4] John, xiv, 8.
[5] John, xiv, 9.
[6] John, xiv, 7.

to lay down His life for them at the end of that time, knowing that, as yet, His very own do not understand Him or appreciate the vast significance of His Person. The truth is that Jesus does nothing from Himself and that the very sustenance of His life is the Will of the Father. The more one studies the way of God, made manifest in the life of Jesus, the more clear does it become that God is satisfied first to do and act and then to hope for recognition of His advances from His creature. Saint John was finally able to express the mystery of the Incarnation thus : "And the Word was made flesh, and dwelt among us . . . " But that was later, when all was over, and when the Spirit of Christ had taken possession of the Church to teach these disciples the real significance of what they had seen with the eyes of their body and loved with the heart of their humanity.

Meanwhile Jesus is content to say that the Spirit, when He comes, will bear testimony to Him. There is something very touching in the way He commits everything to the Father : " I confess to Thee, O Father, Lord of heaven and earth, because Thou hast hid these things from the wise and prudent and hast revealed them to little ones." What Jesus Himself has begun the Spirit will bring to completion. In utter peace He gathers the little ones around Him in the Cenacle ; He gives them the holy Eucharist ; and He speaks to them of the Spirit that is to come. "A little while, and ye behold me no more," He says, "and again a little while and ye shall behold me." The phrasing is enigmatic : they do not understand. " Let not your hearts be troubled," He had begun, thus striking the key-note of all that is to follow : " You believe in God ; believe also in Me." He would hold their loyalty at least, if not their comprehension. As the voices of Thomas, Philip, Judas (not the Iscariot), men usually in the background, are raised in tense, successive inquiries, Jesus sees that He must tell them plainly of His departure. Just when their love for Him is in full tide, He utters the appaling words : " It is expedient for you that I go." Peter asks impulsively : "Whither ? " Jesus answers ; "Whither I go you cannot come." The blow has fallen : there is to be a separation. Loving them as He

did, Jesus could only murmur : "A little while . . . "   For
He would minimise His absence.

Even then the thought of Jesus was fixed upon the
unborn future : in the faces of His disciples He saw the men
and women that God would give Him.   He would depart.
But it was to return again.   As a Man, subject to conditions
of time and place, He irked against these chosen limitations.
He did not belong to Judea alone ; not even to the little faithful
circle now around Him.   He had a mission to all humanity.
If that mission is to be fulfilled, then He must emerge out
of the conditions of time and space and come to men the world
over.   That is why He speaks so insistently to them of the
Spirit that is to come.   With hands uplifted in prayer He says :
" Father, I will that where I am, they also whom Thou hast
given me, may be with me."   He then goes forth to lay down
His life.

II.

It would be an error to imagine that the Apostles fully
entered into everything Jesus said to them at the Last Supper.
They simply did not.   But one thing must have gripped their
minds, the thing expressed in the mysterious phrase that
" they should be where He is, with Him."   From the first
moment they had followed Him, three years before, no thought
ever crossed their minds of leaving Him.   All of them could
have sincerely re-echoed the confession of Peter : " Lord, to
whom shall we go ?   Thou hast the words of eternal life."
It is perfectly evident that Jesus knows this and is only too
anxious to minimise, in every way, the absence that is
necessary.   "A little while, and ye shall behold me no more,"
He said, "And again a little while and ye shall behold me."
Was not this the same as saying that He would go and would
not go ?   The disciples were soon to learn that in this
statement of Jesus there is no contradiction.

There was, however, a subtle thing in the prayer of Jesus
that could easily have escaped their notice. We who know
the sequel are in a position to see it.   It is possible to be where

Jesus is, and yet not be *with Him.* Just as a blind man is where the sun is, though absent from the sun because of his blindness, so may a man be where Jesus is and yet, because of a certain blindness, not be with Him. Saint Augustine makes the point in another connection : "All things are as present to the blind as to the seeing. A blind man and one who hath sight, standing on the same spot, are each surrounded by the same forms of things ; but one is present to them, the other absent."

The whole dramatic interest of this mysterious period is to be found in this antithesis. The possibility of it already lay in the removal of His visible presence. Time only served to bring out into strong relief the meaning of the drama. No sooner had the little group been dispersed than, with one possible exception, each man wandered off into a darkness of his own finding. In that darkness they were soon to learn : He had said He would never go and leave them. The love of Jesus for them, as might have been expected, proved stronger than death. That they should be not only where He is but with Him was, He knew, the vital thing. Therefore immediately after His Resurrection He began to manifest Himself. He, the risen Shepherd of the flock, sent forth His voice into the darkness of His night, calling them back to Him that He might hold them against the day when His Spirit would swoop down upon them from on high to complete their Christian formation and make of them a living Church, an enduring Witness to His presence in the actual world of time and space.

At break of dawn on the first Easter morning, when already the disciples had departed, a woman might have been seen weeping near the sepulchre. As she wept she stooped down looking anxiously into the tomb of death. As she did so, she saw two angels in white, sitting, one at the head and another at the foot, where the Body of Jesus had been laid. Taking compassion on her sorrow, they addressed her : "Woman, why weepest thou ? " Not knowing the facts, she replied : " They have taken away my Lord : and I know not where they have laid Him." At that moment some new awareness on the part of the angels made her turn around. Jesus was standing there. He spoke : "Woman, why weepest thou ? Whom seekest thou ? " Not realising that it was Jesus, the woman said : " Sir, if thou hast taken Him hence, tell me where thou hast laid Him and I will come and take Him away." Then she recalled the two men sitting in the Sepulchre. Turning to them again, she found herself suddenly arrested by the sound of her name, " Mary." Recognition flooded her soul. She threw herself at His feet, saying : " Rabboni." He had a message for her : " Do not touch me . . . but go to my brethren and say to them : I ascend to my Father and to your Father, to my God and to your God."

One has only to ponder on the relation that obtained between Mary Magdalene and our blessed Lord during His public ministry to glimpse some of the significance of this short interview. He had given back to her a soul that she was squandering on the things of sense. Now He was taking her recognition of Him beyond the sacred Humanity which, in life, had drawn her to God. Their relations henceforth will be on the plane of the Spirit and His refusal, just now, to let her touch Him is intended to awaken in her that supernatural desiring which, fanned to flames by the Spirit, will edify the world by the tears of Christian penance. The conversation, whose purport is so clear, is not for Mary alone. It is the way of God to make known His mind to men in society, to brethren, for men are what they are in the sight of God, a people, an assembly of which Jesus is the predestined Head. The sense of a church, so essential a part of the public teaching of our Lord during His ministry on earth, is not absent from this interview on the first Easter morning. Mary was the recipient of a message from the risen Saviour to His brethren.

In this way did He inaugurate the final stage in the spiritual formation of His followers. They were told to expect Him. It is impossible to watch His sudden appearances and disappearances just as sudden, and fail to surmise His purpose. The three essential things in that formation, then as now, are : first, to expand men's minds beyond the narrow world of sense and reason to the vast horizon of the Invisible out of which each time He comes ; second, to purify men's hearts of attachment to the things of earth, which have for effect a binding of the understanding, and to introduce them to the steady light of the Eternal which is His home ; third, to make men realise that they are never to think of Jesus as absent but as always present, preparing them for the advent of the Spirit in Whom He returns to them so that they may have real access to God.

In this way the Master Who insisted that it was expedient for them that He should go was introducing them to an understanding of different modes of presence. He was teaching them that His departure was, in reality, leading to a new, a more intimate presence than they could have enjoyed while He was still visibly in their midst. He was taking their sense of His presence beyond the reach of the senses so that their whole experience, height and extent and depth, should be bound up with Him for Whose sight they now begin to work and wait ; He is offering to their affections a risen Humanity transfused with the light of Godhead so that the love of their hearts shall ever be fixed upon Him who is not only Man but God ; He is transforming the world about them, the world in which they walk, into a new universe, a universe restored to God by the death of Jesus, a universe destined to be the very kingdom of God on earth.

The result will be that, reflecting upon this period of His manifestations to them, the Apostles return to the prayer of Jesus at the Last Supper and find new significance in it. It is possible to be where Jesus is, and yet not be with Him. The difference depends primarily on the Master's own initiative. It is Jesus Who must manifest Himself and if He appears to go away it is with the purpose of drawing near. To those who watch and pray, who are receptive, He reveals Himself and when He does it is with that introduction which so befits Him : " Peace be to you ; it is I, fear not." [1] The disciples were human enough to find that returning

---

[1] Luke, xxiv, 36.

to their daily tasks, without vision of Him, it is easy to slip
back into the narrow world of sense and reason which has
only the advantage for them of being bleak and empty. The
Master wished it so. He was preparing them to be a
House of Light in the darkness of the world. " Now every
house," wrote Saint Paul, "is built by some man . . . but
Christ is the Son in His own house." Our Lord had not
only built the house of the Apostles but to Him it is, in fact,
to belong. And lest we should miss the point, the Apostle
cryptically adds : " Which house are we."

III.

An illustration of the Master's method during this
period is found in the beautiful incident of Emmaus which
took place on the very afternoon of His Resurrection. Two
disciples were turning their backs upon Jerusalem of sacred
memories. It was early afternoon and the setting sun was
shedding lustre about them as they went on their way. But
their appearance contrasted strongly with the glowing
splendour in which they walked : they were downcast and
dispirited. These men had followed the career of Jesus,
and watched its progressive triumph, until that triumph
ended in the darkness of Calvary. Now they were leaving,
with darkness in their minds, and in their hearts the emptiness
of disillusionment.

It was in these conditions a Stranger accosted them.
He was with them, speaking to them, almost before they
realised it : "What are these discourses that you hold one with
another, as you walk," He asked, " and are sad ? " To them
it was incredible that any man should have been in the vicinity
of Jerusalem these last days and not have heard of the events
that took place there. Walking with Him they were absent
from Him, and in this absence the conversation continued.
One of them said to Him : "Art thou only a stranger in
Jerusalem, and hast thou not known the things that have
been done there in these days ? " The Stranger answered :
"What things ? " This gave them an opportunity. They
told Him of Jesus, a Prophet " mighty in work and word

before God and all the people." And it became clear that, for all their enthusiasm, something had happened to their Faith. They had hoped that it was He who should have redeemed Israel. But that hope, it would seem, had vanished since He had been put to death. Of the Resurrection they had tidings only from the women and by these tidings, on their own admission, they were merely " affrighted."

This was a cue for the Stranger Who now chided them for their unbelief. "O foolish and slow of heart, to believe in all things which the prophets have spoken." They were now on common ground. He could argue with them on the basis of the Scriptures. Scripture was filled with the idea of Jesus, of the Man Who would come from God to redeem not only Israel but the nations of the earth. It was true that this idea had suffered at the hands of their interpreters and showed a tendency to break up into two pictures not easy to reconcile : that of a Messiah Who should restore Israel to her rightful place amongst the nations ; and that of a Messiah Who, by suffering, would reconcile humanity to God and make possible the kingdom of God on earth. " It is a small thing," said the Lord to His servant, " that thou shouldest be my servant to raise up the tribes of Jacob, and to convert the dregs of Israel. Behold I have given thee to be the light of the Gentiles . . . " Of Him Isaiah had also written : " Surely he hath borne our infirmities and carried our sorrows . . . But he was wounded for our iniquities, he was bruised for our sins : the chastisement of our peace was upon him and by his bruises we are healed."

That it was this spiritual conception of the Messiah's mission which Jesus now put before them is clear from the question with which He concluded His exposition of " the things that were concerning him." [1] " Ought not Christ to have suffered," He asked, " and so to enter into his glory ? " Referring to all the prophets, as He did, He would have mentioned the prophecy of Isaiah : " For a child is born to us, and a son is given to us, and the government is upon his shoulder : and his name shall be called, Wonderful,

[1] Luke, xxii, 37.

Counsellor, God the Mighty, the Father of the world to come, the Prince of Peace." In Himself Jesus had the right to glory but in death He would, by conquest, acquire the kingdom of humanity. It was fitting, He said, that in such a conquest He should suffer.

The argument was strangely familiar. It brought back memories to them. As they listened their hearts began to stir within them and flames of hope began to issue from the ashes of despair. Just then, as the conversation reached its climax, the falling sun threatened to put an end to it. They had come to the parting of the ways. The Stranger made as if He was about to leave them. A sudden inspiration came to them : they would offer Him hospitality. They began to urge their invitation : " Stay with us, because it is towards evening, and the day is now far spent."

The invitation was accepted ; Jesus went in with them. As they sat down, He took bread into His hands. As He did so, their blindness fell from them. They started up. It was He, the Christ. No sooner had recognition come than Jesus vanished. But the feeling of His presence lingered. Looking back they recognised it : "Was not our heart burning within us, whilst He spoke in the way ? " It mattered little now that the day was "far spent." That very hour they rose up and returned to Jerusalem. Entering in, they told the eleven of their vision. They had scarcely uttered the words when they were privileged again to behold the Master. He stood suddenly in the midst of them. He showed them His hands and feet. He partook of a little fish and honey to convince them that He was no spirit, " for a spirit hath not flesh and bones as you see me to have." He spoke to them. He opened to them the Scriptures. Again they heard the words : " It behoved Christ to suffer and to rise again from the dead." To this had led their meeting with Him on the way to Emmaus when He had spoken to them.

How is it to be explained ? It is only too evident that they did not recognise Him by means of the senses : for these were " held." Nor did they arrive at knowledge of Him by the deductions of their reason because they did not, in fact, draw the conclusion. Recognition came to them before they had time to reason. The only explanation is that Jesus manifested Himself to them. Long before, when Peter had made confession of Him, Jesus traced the origin of this illumination to the Father of all light, and made the contrast between this light and the limitations of " flesh and blood." Here it is the same. It is God alone Who commands the light to shine in the darkness of their hearts " To give the light of the knowledge of the glory of God, in the face of Christ Jesus." [1] It was not that the knowledge of sense and reason had counted for nothing. This had gone before, prepared the way, and it was the self-same Jesus Who now stood revealed. But in this instance, as in the others which mark the period between the Resurrection and Pentecost, recognition came in a flash and the light had its source within the Godhead of Jesus.

IV.

The visible mission of our blessed Lord was at an end. Since His Resurrection He had entered upon a new, a higher plane of existence. If His mission on earth, terminating in the apparent defeat of Calvary, was to succeed, these men must become living witnesses to His presence in the world of space and time : a work as superhuman as redemption lay before them. " I will not leave you orphans," He had said, " I will come to you. Yet a little while ; and the world seeth me no more. But you see me : because I live, and you shall live. In that day you shall know, that I am in my Father, and you in me, and I in you." His final word to them as He rose in majesty from the earth was not to depart from Jerusalem until His promises had been fulfilled.[2]

When at last the cloud hid Him from their watching eyes, and angels in shining garments dismissed them from the heights, they went down from the holy Mount with sacred memories in their hearts. Hopes had come to life within their breasts that may not have been too precise. But it was with

[1] 2 Cor., iv., 6.
[2] Cf. Luke, xxiv, 49.

a vivid sense of expectation that they returned to Jerusalem. It was essentially a time of prayer : by day, in the Temple blessing and praising God ; by night, in the Upper Room so hallowed by the memory of the Eucharist. In this way, at the bidding of their Master, they awaited the decisive miracle of their transformation. This Upper Room now housed, in the midst of universal corruption, the hope of the world's peace : a little gathering with Mary, the Mother of Jesus, in their midst. The official priesthood of the Temple considered it a duty to prepare, as of old, for the visitation of the Most High. In due time the day of manifestation, the fifteenth after Pasch, dawned. In the early morning the priests of the Temple were engaged in offering the first fruits of the harvest. The disciples had not left the Upper Room. Before they could do so, the Miracle of Pentecost took place. The God Who, in other days, had filled the Temple with the cloud of His majestic presence now descended upon the Upper Room.

No human words could adequately describe the event. Holy Scripture relates it in the simplest terms : " And suddenly there came a sound from heaven, as of a mighty wind coming, and it filled the whole house where they were sitting. And there appeared to them parted tongues of fire, and it sat upon every one of them.[1] Never in the history of the Chosen People had there been such an out-pouring of the Spirit of God. The living Flame of God's own Love, the Spirit of Christ, had taken possession of them. It was a veritable baptism of fire, as the Baptist had foretold, and suddenly they realised that Jesus had come back to earth to realise the kingdom that must enfold within its Peace the far-flung nations of the earth.

The effects were stupendous and immediate. Within this Presence they felt themselves effaced, but in that self-effacement they experienced the power of God. New horizons opened up before their minds ; their hearts were bursting with some new tide of love ; in their very bodies they felt the Spirit urging and compelling them " to utter

[1] Acts, ii, 2.

speech in divers tongues." Caught up in the tumult of this
visitation, the little group could not contain itself ; voices
were raised in an ecstacy of joy.   Soon a crowd had gathered.
The city was filled with " pious and godfearing Jews from
every nation under heaven."   Hearing songs of jubilation,
people hurried to see ; they climbed the stairs that led to
the Upper Room.   The sight that met their gaze was
unforgetable :   an entire group in ecstacy, exulting in the
wonders of the Lord, and to the listeners' consternation each
one, no matter the land or idiom of his origin, could
understand what was being uttered.

Affrighted by the miracle, they asked : "What does this
mean ?   Are not these Galileans ? "   The pious marvelled ;
the wicked scoffed.   Wickedness found its tongue of mockery :
" These people are drunk and are filled with sweet wine."
In a sense it was true.   The little group was intoxicated
with the mystic wine of Jesus.   Coming out of ecstacy Peter
explained.   A promise had been made by Jesus.   He said He
would not leave them orphans : " Behold I am with you all
days even to the consummation of the world."   Literally the
promise had just been fulfilled.   Jesus had come to them in
His Spirit to form the Church and to "convince the world of
sin, and of justice, and of judgment " : of sin, because the
world has not accepted Jesus ; of justice, because there is
no holiness which is not a sharing in the holiness of Jesus ;
of judgment, because the destiny of men shall be decided by
their attitude to Jesus.   Just when His enemies thought they
had annihilated and destroyed the Christ, Jesus returns,
more victorious than ever, to inhabit that new, that mystic
Body which is the Church of God on earth.   Where Jesus is,
there also is Peace : " These things I have spoken to you,
that in me you may have peace.   In the world you shall have
distress : but have confidence, I have overcome the world." [1]

[1] John, xvi. 33.

IX.

Holiness.

I.

There can be no constructive thinking about holiness without the light of the ideal to guide our thought. It is the ideal which, in every sphere, gives meaning to the actual. Things exist not only to be what they are, at any given moment, but to increase their likeness to the ideal which God has in mind for them. This is particularly true of man. So supremely excellent is God's ideal for him that we have no conception of it until we raise our minds to Jesus. Our blessed Lord is not only the Son of God but the Son of Man—the new Adam Who is the perfect prototype of all holiness. In Him the entire complacency of God is centred and the ideal for man is that he should be re-made in the image and likeness of the Perfect, Jesus.

If we would enter into this divine design, we must appeal to a mind before which the plan of God, in all its splendour, unfolds itself. Our choice must be, in the first instance, Jesus Himself and, then, those minds into which He poured the light of His own vision. It was characteristic of our Lord to express the sublimest truths in the simplest way. Truths beyond the mind's capacity to understand He would clothe in images of daily life. When He wished, for instance, to expound the precise relationship between the grace of God and the souls of men, He enunciated the parable of the Sower.[1] Nothing could be at once more simple and sublime where grace is shown for what it is—the seed of eternal life sown in the

[1] Mark, iv, 3.

124

soil of human souls.   The more this parable is pondered over
and penetrated, the more exactly is the relation between grace
and nature understood.   Grace is a beginning made in eternal
life, a vital seed whose intrinsic energy is divine, while its
growth is made dependent upon the soil of human nature
where it germinates.   When Jesus spoke of casting fire upon
the earth, in another sublime image, the earth He had in mind
was that of human nature which is to be caught up in the flame
of His Holy Spirit.

It is remarkable, in fact, how frequently our blessed
Lord reverts to this image, or similar ones, in His anxiety
to bring home to His hearers the initiative of God in
communicating supernatural life to humanity.   Jesus has in
mind the exact vision of God's own dream, for the perfection
of human personality.   At the Last Supper, when His disciples
were gathered around Him, He said : "Amen, amen, I say to
you, unless the grain of wheat falling into the ground die,
itself remaineth alone.   But if it die, it bringeth forth much
fruit." [1]   The phrasing of that magnificent statement is
significant.   No man could have lived long in the company of
Jesus and imagine that it was His ambition to remain alone.
It is true that we can appreciate a love which is in need of
receiving better than that which is in need of giving, but it
must be realised that there is a love which calls for society
more even for what it can give than for what it can receive.
The need which Jesus experienced was the need of giving.
Had He not called, and gathered, disciples to Him ?   Had He
not gladly suffered them, for three whole years, bearing with
their limitations and their imperfect understanding of Him ?
Was He not just on the point of instituting the sacrament of
their union with Him, and in Him, with one another ?   Saint
John, who had entered deeply into His intentions, says :
" Having loved his own who were in the world, he loved them
to the end." [2]   And as Jesus looked Godwards, there was
another thought impelling Him in the same direction.   The
homage of His death, which He was willing to offer, would be
worthy of recompense : "Ask of me and I will give thee the

[1] John, xii, 24.
[2] John, xiii, 1.

gentiles for thy inheritance." ¹   Jesus was Himself to be the
very Source of life for the world to come.

Our blessed Lord was thinking, on that night, of the
Mystic Vine He declared Himself to be whose branches would
be His followers in every age : " I am the Vine, you are the
branches : he that abideth in Me, and I in him, the same
beareth much fruit, for without Me you can do nothing." ²
This is an image of surpassing beauty, whose spiritual
significance is inexhaustible.   The roots of the Vine, plunging
into Godhead, would draw abundant life for the branches.
The whole Tree, root and branch and blossom, would be a
living unity : "Abide in me and I in you.   As the branch
cannot bear fruit of itself, unless it abide in the vine, so neither
can you, unless you abide in me." ³   Before His eyes rose up
the spectacle of that marvellous transformation by which the
tree of death, the Cross of the morrow, would blossom into
life, spreading forth its branches in all directions, and offering
to generations as yet unborn the fruits of eternal life : " I sat
down under His shadow whom I desired : and his fruit was
sweet to my palate." ⁴

His prophecy of death was fulfilled in the apparent
defeat of Calvary.   But by that defeat Jesus prepared His
triumph.   Like the Good Shepherd that He was, the risen
Saviour sent out His voice into the night of the scattered
apostles calling them back to Him against the day of their
common triumph.   " For John indeed," He told them,
" baptised you with water, but you shall be baptised with the
Holy Ghost, not many days hence." ⁵   The gift of His Spirit
Jesus had also promised at the Last Supper.   He would be
present to them both in the Flesh and in the Spirit.   Think
of it.   This was the Spirit Who had overshadowed Mary for
the conception of Jesus in His human nature, the Spirit Who
had imparted to the humanity of our Lord that " fulness of

---

¹ Ps., ii, 8.
² John, xv, 5.
³ John, xv, 4.
⁴ Canticle, ii, 3.
⁵ Acts, i, 5.

grace " of which all were to receive, the very Spirit in Whose power He had accomplished all He had done for the salvation of mankind and Who was the living Inspiration of all His ways. By means of the Holy Spirit, Who is God's Gift of gifts, at once collective and individual, Jesus would inaugurate that mystic phase of His existence on earth which is the real source and secret of Christian holiness.

At Pentecost the promise made by Jesus was fulfilled. Pentecost was, in fact, the decisive miracle in the birth of Christianity. " The Church already conceived," wrote Pope Leo XIII, " was born from the side of the second Adam as He slept on the Cross ; and it was clearly manifested to the eyes of men on the solemn day of Pentecost." [1] The gospel of fire that burst upon the gathered disciples in the Upper Room revealed to them the true mission of Jesus in all its extent and meaning. They realised the truth of the Master's image. It was as if the branches, suddenly becoming aware of their true life, experienced their mysterious unity with the Vine. The value of an image however, must not be obscured by taking literally what the image is intended figuratively to convey. When our Lord spoke of Himself as the Vine of which His followers are the branches, He wished to express a union with Him which is not incompatible with the distinctiveness of human personality. The Holy Father, Pius XII, has found it necessary, in that magnificent document *Mystici Corporis Christi*, to exclude a misunderstanding which would make " Christ our Lord subject to human error and human frailty." The fact is that the union in question is a " mystic " union, which is neither physical nor merely moral, and which is an invitation to men to exercise themselves " in works of holiness." Just as in the original image of the seed which falls into the ground the soil itself contributes to the birth of life, and its development, so in the life of holiness man must do his part if the grace of God is to fructify in good works. " The grace of God," said Saint Paul, " in me hath not been vain ; but I have laboured more abundantly than all they. Yet not I, but the grace of God with me." [2]

[1] Enc. *Divinum Illud.*
[2] 1 Cor., xv, 10.

II.

So important is this truth of the mystic union between Christ and Christians for an understanding of holiness that we may briefly look at it from another point of view. To Saint Paul was given a very vivid understanding of this truth and it is characteristic of him that he is able, at any moment, to suggest the integral truth of Christianity. He enjoys that priceless gift, a living inspiration, which unifies the energies of his mind. Rays of that vision, for which the very meaning of life is Christ, light up his every page and a single phrase, taken almost at random, can fill his reader's mind with light. One such phrase tells of the purpose of God " to re-establish all things in Christ, that are in heaven and on earth, in him." [1] At a bound the mind is taken up into the heart of God in which the Apostle reads the secret of His purpose ; from there it surveys the majestic climax of a final achievement, a summing up in which all things, whether on earth or in heaven, are brought under the immediate Headship of Jesus Christ.

This Headship of our blessed Saviour is the constant theme of Saint Paul. He sees the Church, of which Jesus is the Head as a Body ; and together they form what Saint Thomas designates " one mystic Person." This is, in truth, " the mystery which hath been hidden from ages and generations, but now is manifested to his saints." [2] Nor are we doing violence to the text in applying to the Church what the Apostle affirms historically of Christ. The whole context justifies us. The mystery hidden from the ages, and from those who are dominated by the spirit of the world, is that Jesus still lives upon the earth, building up that new, that mystic Body of which we are members, so that an eternal dream of God is in the process of realisation by the agency of His Spirit. That dream is a humanity re-made " in the image and likeness of God," " for whom He foreknew He also predestinated to be made comformable to the image of his Son." [3] In Him we were chosen " unto the praise of his

---

[1] Eph., I, 10.

[2] Roms., xvi. 25.

[3] Roms., viii, 29.

glory," [1] before the creation of the world, so that "we shall be holy and unspotted in his sight, in charity." [2] Now "God is charity" [3] and it is contact with God, to Whom we have access in the Spirit of Christ, which alone can render men " holy and unspotted " in His eyes.

This allows us to make a distinction which is fundamental in any discussion of holiness. There is, first, a holiness of being, a state of sanctity, by which man is graced by God and made a sharer in His Life. There is, secondly, a holiness of action, of conduct, in which the renovated being of man expresses itself in good works. The first form of holiness is sanctifying grace, something essentially hidden ; the second may reveal itself in a heroism of action and is, to that extent, visible. But it often happens that appearances are deceptive ; many men are holy who do not seem to be ; some seem holy who are really not. The essential thing is sanctifying grace ; and grace is not visible to the naked eye or the natural mind. By grace a man is " born of God," as Saint John says, and to be " born of God " means a mysterious sharing in the Sonship of Jesus. The little child, just baptised, possesses an essential holiness long before it is capable of human actions.

The holiness of baptismal grace, which is truly sanctifying, is the first condition of Christian Holiness. Like all beginnings it contains in germ the full development of a life of holiness. Did we appreciate, as we ought, the meaning of sanctifying grace we should see that holiness is our fundamental obligation. " By grace," said Saint Bonaventure, " the soul has become the child of the Father, the spouse of the Word, and the temple of the Holy Spirit." This points to ineffable relations to each of the Three Persons, dwelling in the soul, which only the life of holiness itself can make clear. We can have no adequate conception, at present, of the joy that fills the heart of God when He finds His heaven within the soul of a new humanity and beholds the glory of His Son radiating from human nature regenerated in the waters of Baptism.

---

[1] Eph., 1, 12.
[2] Eph., 1, 4.
[3] 1 John, iv, 8.

Throughout the Church, which is one, He seeks this glory : in heaven, where, in the abyss of joy, the blessed know God " even as they are known " ; in purgatory, where hunger for His sight, amidst the purifying flames, is but a response to God's own longing ; on earth, where men seek God because He has found them, having called them to fellowship with His Son, Jesus. God has found in Jesus the way in which to reunite men, and through men all creatures, to Himself so that He can love in suffering and humble humanity the Infinitude which is the proper object of His love. Equally certain is it that in Jesus alone humanity can offer to God the praise and honour which are His due. For that reason the ultimate formula of holiness can only be that inexhaustible text of Saint Paul : "And I live, now not I ; but Christ liveth in me." The Christian ideal lies hidden in these words.

III.

The ideal serves not only as an inspiration but as a beacon to light the way of holiness in. action. Let the Christian ideal in all its divine attractiveness once grip the mind and the cost were little. To realise that it is Jesus Who wants to live in us, to take possession of our minds and bodies and spirits, is to experience that need of giving which He alone draws forth in its fullest glory. An ideal so exalted makes demands upon the man who accepts it. These demands may be gathered into one and written down as a veritable law of life. Our blessed Lord took care to formulate this law, for He said to all : "If any man will come after me, let him deny himself, and take up his cross daily and follow me. For whosoever shall save his life shall lose it, and he that shall lose his life for my sake shall save it." To live to Christ a man must die to self. Self-sacrifice is the condition of entry into the kingdom of God on earth.

This was to be expected. If Jesus is to live anew, by grace in humanity then radical autonomy of the human self is out of the question. But the man who surrenders to Christ accepts the Spirit of Christ and loses his life only to gain it. A strict proportion exists between this loss and gain so that as self surrenders, the empire of Jesus as another Self progressively

increases. Saint Paul was well aware of this when he wrote :
" For which cause we faint not ; but though the outward man
is corrupted, yet the inward man is renewed day by day." If
Jesus wishes to nourish Himself upon the substance of a human
life then the man who surrenders to Him will find that he
himself is nourished upon the Bread of Godhead. It is a fact
of history, verified in the lives of Christian saints, that the
secret of holiness is to be found in the law which says that a
man who would save his life must lose it in the larger Life of
Godhead to which access is given by Jesus Christ.

This law was not formulated by our Lord without being
first consecrated by His own life and action. He was, Himself,
the most complete expression of it. He was the holy One of
God in Whom no human self disputed the empire of God,
Whose human will was ever in harmony with the divine, and
He died to Himself in poverty, chastity and obedience upon
the Cross of Calvary. Renunciation implies suffering.
Jesus did not flinch before the prospect. When towards
the end He said " I come forth from the Father and am
come into the world ; again I leave the world and go to the
Father," He was on His way to the sacrifice by which
He would consecrate in His Blood the law of life. The
order of things first brought into being by creative Love
excluded suffering which now we associate with self-sacrifice :
suffering then existed only as a menace and a threat. In such a
state of bliss holiness would have flowered and blossomed as
spontaneously as the lily decks itself with beauty. But that
order exists no longer. The consequence is that the rebirth
of holiness, and its growth, is not without its measure of
suffering.

The incorporation of a man with Jesus, which results from
Baptism, implies a sharing in a life whose law is sacrifice.
An order of things that takes its rise in the Cross is governed
by the Cross. This is true not only of our Lord in His
natural Body but of our Lord in His mystic Body. That is
why in a sinful world the saving influence of the Church, His
mystic Body, is so necessary. Now there is not a single
manifestation of the life of the Church on earth, be it dogma,

morals, or liturgy, which is not sealed with the Cross. The Cross is now the Tree of Life. And if it is true that man's life is like a tree planted in the earth, then sacrifice is the law of its growth. But sacrifice and suffering go together. Of our blessed Lord Saint Bonaventure said : " He was the fruit of Mary's virginity Who on the Cross reached maturity beneath the Sun of divine Justice." To be incorporated with Him, by grace, is to be nailed to that Cross from which mystics, on earth have looked into the depths of heaven. The happiness of heaven is no mere human bliss but a sharing in the bliss of God. The Apocalypse makes the promise : " To him, that overcometh, I will give to eat the tree of life, which is in the paradise of God."

All life is at once a doing and a suffering ; and love lies at the source of both. To His followers Jesus offers His Heart by means of grace, to be the beating pulse of their lives : " who hath sealed us, and given the pledge of the Spirit in our hearts." Some are called especially to suffering and what they have to remember is that to live well all that is required is to love well and love is proved in suffering. To them our Lord makes known a secret joy, the joy of suffering, which He alone can give : this joy He has stored up for those with whom, and in whom, He suffers. It is the age-long experience of the Church on earth that heroism of virtue belongs not only to lives of action but lives of suffering and that each progressive phase of holiness has its own specific form of suffering. For if the life of holiness begins amidst the difficulties and sacrifices of the ascetical life, preparing man in successive purification for the life of union, a moment comes when a man suffers rather because he loves than because he wants to love. The path of progress from humble beginnings to highest sanctity is one continuous witness to the increasing pressure of Jesus, Who by the power of His Spirit, awakens and intensifies a man's docility to His influence : " For whosoever are led by the Spirit of God, those are the sons of God." Nothing less is implied by fellowship with Jesus Who is " head over all the Church, which is his body, and the fulness of him, who is filled all in all." [1]

[1] Eph., 1, 23.

IV.

A simple scene from the Gospel will serve to relate these thoughts to the immediate needs of practice for the ordinary life of action. Our blessed Lord was tender-hearted. It could not have been otherwise in One Who possessed the Heart of a woman. He was touched by the sight of human misery in which He saw the shadow cast by sin. Having come to roll back that shadow, He frequently exercised His power over human maladies, with the implicit injunction not to sin again. On one occasion a deaf-mute was led before Him. The Master was touched by this spectacle of silent misery. He took the man apart, put His fingers in his ears, and moistening them He touched the man's tongue. The effect was instantaneous : the man heard. The first sound that filled the newly-awakened world of his consciousness was the exultant voice of the enthusiastic multitude : " Behold, he hath done all things well." [1] The more the Master tried to reduce their enthusiasm to true proportions, the more strength the voices gathered in acclamation.

This was a very human crowd. Men are naturally impressed by miraculous deeds and by spectacular manifestations. Never, it is true, was praise more merited. But it was not precisely for the reason that inspired the crowd led, as it was, more by imagination than by reflection. This act of Jesus was great not because it was a miracle but precisely because it was the act of Jesus. It is precisely what Jesus is, God expressing Himself in human form, which gives value, divine value, to His every action. In the bosom of Godhead the word is the Praise and the Glory of God ; on earth the incarnate Word is the manifestation of God in time. Had the crowd been able to reflect, in the light of Faith, it would have known that every action of Jesus, God as well as Man, is perfect. Jesus, in fact, has sanctified the common-place. He lived a human life. He ate and drank and worked and slept. Therefore, to eat and drink, to work and sleep can now be divine actions in one Who is incorporated, by grace, with Jesus.

If every act of Jesus whether in His natural or His mystic Body is divine, then we can see the elemental condition of

[1] Mark, vii, 37.

holiness. But if every act of Jesus is divine, there is also a standard and a norm by which He regulates His actions. That standard, now as during his earthly ministry, is the sovereign Will of God. From the first moment of His existence in time to the last moments when He accepted the bitter chalice of His passion, Jesus declared that the very food and nourishment of His life is the Will of God. This will finds expression for Him in the Cross by which He will save the world for God. Now it is possible for every Christian to find in the duties of his state in life the Cross by which, in union with His Master, he can sanctify himself. There are different kinds of duty but before that particular duty which is God's Will, as it finds expression in the changing circumstances of time, all men are equal : duty is the cross that every Christian must take up. And it is by bearing the cross of duty, perhaps modest and not spectacular, which has the advantages of being at once real and monotonous, that a man is graced with real holiness.

If with Jesus His true followers form what Saint Thomas has not feared to designate as " one mystic Person," then the obligation of conformity with Him in the actual present is evident. This conformity must be understood. It is not a question merely of copying an external model but rather of allowing the Spirit of Christ to overshadow us with His vivifying influence. The better to dispose ourselves for this influence we must endeavour to think and desire and act as Jesus would. The ultimate effect of the reciprocal love which is born of such commerce will be that, instinctively, we shall act in every circumstance in such a way that the signature of Jesus may be written to our every thought, desire and action. That so sublime an ideal is not beyond our powers we owe to Jesus, Who, sharing with His church the Spirit of holiness, has placed within the reach of His followers an infallible Instinct to urge, impel, and guide them in the greatest art of all—the art of living. To be docile to the Spirit of Christ is to be engaged in building up that Temple of Eternity, the mystic Body, to the full measure of God's design so that 'doing the truth in love, we may grow in all things in Him Who is Head, Christ. To be a perfect man . . . '[1]

[1] Cf. Eph., iv, 11–15.